RHYMES, CRIMES
and
OTHER PASTIMES

RHYMES, CRIMES, and *OTHER PASTIMES*

Brett Gordon

RESOURCE *Publications* • Eugene, Oregon

RHYMES, CRIMES, AND OTHER PASTIMES

Copyright © 2021 Brett Gordon. All rights reserved. Except for brief quotations in critical publications or reviews, no part of this book may be reproduced in any manner without prior written permission from the publisher. Write: Permissions, Wipf and Stock Publishers, 199 W. 8th Ave., Suite 3, Eugene, OR 97401.

Resource Publications
An Imprint of Wipf and Stock Publishers
199 W. 8th Ave., Suite 3
Eugene, OR 97401

www.wipfandstock.com

PAPERBACK ISBN: 978-1-6667-3486-7
HARDCOVER ISBN: 978-1-6667-9123-5
EBOOK ISBN: 978-1-6667-9124-2

November 12, 2021 1:06 PM

The characters and events portrayed in this book are fictitious. Any similarity to real persons, living or dead, is coincidental and not intended by the author.

Dedicated to my son, Bruce Ian Gordon, for his persistent encouragement over the years to compile my selected poems and short stories into a single volume.

Contents

RHYMES

The Ballad of Irving Butterfield | 3
Howard Hasty's Request | 5
The Mail of Eldred Straw | 6
Homer Thwing | 7
Cabin Fever Blues | 8
The Tooth Fairy | 10
Winslow Grey and Side-Stepping Willy | 12
The Growth on Harold | 14
Otis Saturday | 16
The Employment of Freddy and Ralph | 17
The Laziness of William Tooley | 18
The Loathing for Simon Sullivan | 20
The Plumbing of Tolliver Hayes | 22
The Town Drunk | 23
The Sleeplessness of George | 24
The Birthdays of Lester Fothergill | 25
My Friend, Brian | 26
An Ode for the Porcelain Throne | 27
Bloody Bones, the Ogre | 28

A Hanging | 30
The Ghost of Til-Gaviel | 32
The Epitaphs of Alfie Baker and Stanley Cook | 35
The Trees | 36
In Memory of Cora and Walter Bean | 38
The Court Jester | 40
The Beast Beneath My Bed | 42
The Ballad of Molly and Dale | 43
The Insatiable Hunger of Jethro Hapgood | 44
Alice Thatcher | 46
The Village Idiot | 47
The Phantoms of Bulwark Castle | 48
The Retirement of Malcolm McCready | 50
The Bride of Halliwell Hall | 51

CRIMES

Dio | 55
Where Do Flies Go at Night? | 111
All That Glitters | 118
Combustible | 122
Matthew | 135
Hagberry Pot | 140
They Come Back | 146
The River | 155
Worm Food | 159
Twisted | 165
Second Sight | 175

OTHER PASTIMES

A Flower | 197
A Moth | 198
Gothic Desire | 199
Oceanic Aerosol | 200
Lament of a Fallen Angel | 201
Civil Duty and Circus Tents | 202
Balloon | 204
Friends | 205
Sentimental Incense | 206
Nothing Can Stop Us Now | 208
The Ocean's Wrath | 210
September Song | 211
Then | 212
American Mexico | 214
Dreams | 216
Infinite Sadness | 217
Farming | 218
Iron | 219
Eden | 220
Hourglass | 222
Always | 225
Transient Mirrors | 227
Roman | 228
Another Holocaust | 230
Butterflies | 231

In Green Pastures | 232
The Mist Amang the Heather | 233
There Was a Garden Once | 234
October | 236
The Most Beautiful Suicide | 237
Intervals | 239
Another Day at the Races | 240
Forgotten | 241
Send in the Clowns | 242
Matthew 6:34 | 243
Star Blood | 244
The Twilight of This Evening | 245
My Verdict | 246
Wind | 248
My Love | 249
Bydand | 250
Last Thoughts | 251

RHYMES

The Ballad of Irving Butterfield

Irving Butterfield was a good man, some would say,
Except when he strolled across someone's way.
His smell was as foul as an odor goes—
A body unwashed, and in a pig farmer's clothes.

He bathed in a tub about once every year
To wash off the dirt that would otherwise adhere.
Once, in Snaggle-tooth Annie's bath house, he bathed,
And from the filth remaining, he had to be saved.

He would join the children in their afternoon play,
For no one made a mud pie better than him anyway,
But their mothers demanded that justice be carried out,
And finally, one day, the judge proceeded to shout:

"Irving, I order you to bathe at least once every week.
You will wash your body from your head to your feet,
No longer are you to walk our streets in disgust,
This court so orders you, for these words are just!"

Passing by the townsfolk as he made his way out,
They laughed in his face, scrambling about.
The children he played with, the kids that he loved,
Spat upon his face as they pushed and shoved.

Those shimmering eyes that he thought he once knew,
Made him now realize what he must do,
So, in shame and sadness, he picked up his pace,
And made his way homeward, covering his face.

For three days in his absence the townsfolk made jokes
Of Irving Butterfield's filth and his loathing of soaks,
But after a week, when all the commotion died down,
They realized they had not seen Irving around town.

Then during his sermon one Sabbath, the Pastor spoke,
"One should not hate another who dislikes soap!"
So, they repented of the hatefulness each one had sown,
And marched to Irving's pig farm, which was his home.

Upon a mat of straw in the corner of his shack,
Appeared the body of Irving, flat on his back.
In filth he remained except for the cheeks of his face,
Where the bitter tears ran down, now without trace.

Irving Butterfield never asked for very much—
He simply chose to live without a woman's touch.
He was a man unto himself, who lived without vice,
But for his love of filth, he paid a great price.

Let us learn something good from this unhappy affair,
For each of us all have our own crosses to bear.
One should not hurt another, nor jeer or laugh,
Lest we too find ourselves on that sad, lonely path.

Howard Hasty's Request

Howard Hasty came to my house one day,
With his head downcast, and his pockets empty.
It seemed he was in the need of a place to stay,
So, he reminded me of the mule he once lent me.

"Out of my abode, my wife threw me,
Out of my home, and into the street!
Without a room for a day and twenty,
And for eleven, nothing to eat!"

It was out of pity that he became my guest,
But I was coughing at the door within the week.
He overstayed his welcome, and I must confess,
His appetite left me very little to eat.

Then at last, on my doorstep, did he stand,
Both of his cheeks healthier than mine!
He said that he would never understand
Why some must suffer the likes of his kind.

Yet, grateful he was, as he slapped my back,
And with a skip, he was back on his way.
Left my house was—in a state of lack—
Empty of food that I had locked away.

For all these words, I find nothing learned,
But for the knowledge of a deed well done.
'Tis nothing gained, and even less to be earned,
And if you seek advice, I can give you none.

All I can say, and with the fullness of heart,
Is that you help your neighbor, whatever the cost.
If you cannot help a friend from the very start,
If he loses, then I suppose you too are lost.

The Mail of Eldred Straw

That old drifter, Eldred Straw, was just the type
To spend hours on a porch, smoking a pipe,
But it was never his own porch where he'd sit.
It was someone else's where his match was lit!

I thought he lived up near Baboosic Lake Road,
But he only had a camp there, or so I was told.
He was a Merrimack fireman for 60 odd years,
Then he retired, though he still volunteers.

Without a working organ in his flea-bitten frame,
He managed to remember everyone by name.
When delivering mail to him from his niece in Hoboken,
I'd hear that familiar cough from too much smokin'.

"G'mornin', Mr. Post Man," he would cheerfully shout,
Pulling away his pipe from his whiskered mouth.
"Jus' bidin' my time, taking in all this fresh air
From this 'ol porch of mine in my favorite chair!"

An hour later, as I continued to walk my beat,
I'd catch him smoking from a porch on Meadow Street.
There he'd sit, with his dirty boots up on a rail,
Drinking from someone's milk bottle, reading their mail.

Eldred Straw was a confused, but harmless old gent,
Who misunderstood where his mail was being sent.
For a year or so after he was sometime dead,
His niece found 400 unopened letters beneath his bed.

I miss that old man; I used to see him several times a day
When delivering my mail all along the way.
It seems he was the only person whom I ever caught
Waving to me from a porch, whether it was his, or not.

Homer Thwing

Homer Thwing was a poor bum, not self-proclaimed,
Who took desperate measures to change his name.
He tried the town 'Registry of Naming' first,
But they offered him a name that was ten times worse!

So, to the streets he returned, a sad, broken man,
Trying to express his plight so that all might understand,
"It ain't my fault! It ain't my fault!" he would say,
"It was the church that baptized me in this way!"

But no one listened, because nobody cared,
For it was the humor in his name that everyone shared.
"Who'd name a child, 'Homer Thwing?' many asked,
No wonder he drowned himself in a whiskey flask."

Cabin Fever Blues

Got locked inside the other day,
'just doing what I've been told.
Now it looks like I'm here to stay,
Warm and safe from the cold.

Not much on the television,
I don't have one anyway.
My home is more like a prison,
Since being shut in night and day.

I'm running low on beans and pork,
I ran out of patience long ago.
A lotta folks still dying in New York,
'gonna sing about it on my 'ol banjo.

Fixin' to spend more time in bed
To sleep away these empty days.
Not much hope looking ahead,
Behind me, or even sideways.

I think I've been forgotten—
Isolation being good for the soul?
Except now all my food is rotten
And I'm down to my last toilet roll.

As the world is dying off
From this ailment from hell,
At least I ain't got the cough
And I still feel pretty well.

What's the good in dying
If I can't get out through this door?
What's the good in trying
Unless I know what I'm doing it for.

Too afraid to go outside,
Too bored to remain indoors,
But this cabin—still occupied—
Isn't mine and it isn't yours.

Though safe from the world, I feel dead
As long as I remain in this tiny room.
Cabin fever is worse than the dread
Of a world that still exists in doom.

The Tooth Fairy

Childhood belief in fairies, bunnies, Santa and elves,
Though not genuine, each have a kernel of truth.
Of all the fairy tale books on their bedroom shelves,
The one they can believe in, is the one with the tooth.

Every fairy tale originates from some corner of the world:
Trolls in Norway, English pixies, and Giants from Gath.
Some of them are kind—especially to a boy or a girl,
But others can be nasty, vindictive, and full of wrath.

Fairies are a mix of mischief, benevolence, and fun,
Some will be your friend, but there are others that kill.
The search for these pixies is not for everyone.
Such journeys we know of have made many men ill.

Once such story, one such tale—a real fairy tale in fact—
Concerns a man from the west Cornish town of Tintagel.
He was a cobbler for many years before he got sacked,
Lost all hope, and fell under a bewitching spell.

This man loved gold better than the drunk his beer,
More than the libertine his love of women and a tune.
His quest was for the gold that he believed was more near
Than over the hills and far away under the Harvest moon.

He would need to sneak up on one of their midnight revels,
Taking great care to remain silent and unseen.
These fairies were beautiful, but they were really devils,
Destroying those who endeavored to intervene.

He climbed the fairy hill and settled down for the night,
The night was so clear, he could see each blade of grass.
Gazing upon them, he was given a great fright,
When he was startled by a glowing, enchanted lass.

Gazing into her eyes, he fell asleep among the willow,
And when he awoke with his gold, his teeth were gone.
To this day, each child who hides a tooth beneath a pillow
Awakes with hidden money the very next dawn.

Winslow Grey and Side-Stepping Willy

Winslow Grey limped into town one day
With a dead man slung across his back.
He laid him over a rail along the way
As he kept an eye open for an attack.

Through his nostrils he blew the smoke
Of a stale and soggy cigarette.
Although he was half-starved and broke,
Across the Saloon bar he laid a bet.

"I can shoot the ear from a fly
Whilst in mid-flight, lost in the dark.
I will leave no trace for the human eye
To find it nothin' but blown apart."

Silence filled the smoky, foul place
For a moment, or perhaps two, at the most.
Then from the corner emerged a face,
Uglier than sin, that no man would boast.

He was known as Side-Stepping Willy,
And he was not a man to bet.
He made Winslow look a little bit silly
When he took a stand and made his threat.

One could say that he's 'been around'
And that he's had his share of the ladies.
He's sent many a man into the ground,
And they all wait for him in Hades.

Side-Stepping Willy finally moseyed over
And blew a ring of smoke in Winslow's eyes.
Winslow blinked as though he was sober
And said, "What about them bloody flies?"

Side-Stepper replied that he had bigger game
So, he laid his money on the bar.
Winslow hung his arm around some dame
And covered it with his Sherriff's star.

"If you win, you've got my job and pay
And the rightful claim to wear my badge,
But you'll leave yer money with me today
When I win this bet from our little match."

"Just tell me what your game is
And you'll join that there body outside,
For dying is just the same as
Loosing when you cannot abide."

Then with Winslow's closing words of warning,
Side-Stepper shot him in the loins,
And before the dawn of the next morning,
Winslow's eyes were filled with coins.

The moral of this sad tale of late
Is that to kill, is only to be killed.
If it's glory that you seek from fate,
Then you too may get your own eyes filled.

The Growth on Harold

Harold's growth seemed to be faring well,
Until one day when he slipped and fell.
The growth enlarged, and little hairs soon sprouted,
And all was well, until his wife finally shouted:

"What is that ugly growth upon yer brow?
It ain't exactly attractive to me anyhow.
I've been yer wife all of these years,
Workin' and slavin' just like a beast,
So, let me cut it off over a couple of beers
And make all of this growth-sprouting cease!"

"But my dear," Harold sheepishly replied,
"It simply ain't my fault . . .
Please don't forsake me,
And take this all with a grain 'o salt.
The time will come when I'll be dead,
And you will be left on your own
Eatin' only butter on bread,
With soup made from a chicken bone.

"We all have our faults and growths
To deal with in our troubled lives—
Some of us grin and bear 'em, while others
Chop away at 'em with pocketknives.
If you cannot take me for what I'm worth—
Growths, warts, skin tags, and all—
Then shut your gob, lest I make you part
Of our dining room wall!"

"Threatening me with a knock-a-bout,
Ain't no way to treat a bride from yer youth,
Especially with you bald-headed in the mouth
Without a single workin' tooth!
You're as fat as a hog and lame as an ass,
'An there's so little of you that I ever ask.
I ain't gonna take to that growth on yer head,
'Coz there ain't enough room for it in our bed!"

So, with that, Harold's wife struck a nerve,
Because he was never going to sleep on the floor.
With the strength he had left, still on reserve,
He avoided a lengthy row, another war.
He yielded like one of his sheep before the slaughter
And drank a gallon of whiskey like it was water.
Harold's wife hacked away with great aim,
But when he awoke, he was never the same.

The moral of this story, the point of this tale,
Is some arguments with the wife are going to fail.
Though the growth on Harold was faring well,
To his wife, it still looked like a thing from hell.
A little blood spilt to make another delighted,
Perhaps isn't so bad, or even short-sighted.
Better to sleep with your wife, than on your own,
Especially over a growth made of skin and bone.

Otis Saturday

Otis Saturday was born in 1930 at the age of two,
A child beyond his years, and those of his parents, too.
He played piano, aged three, and wore a fez.
He was gifted beyond his years—everyone says.

By the time he was four, he wanted much more
Than the vermin his folks caught in a dinner trap.
He was a talented boy not knowing he was poor,
And subjected to starvation and his father's strap.

Pick up your smiles from the floor and run,
Legends have been made up and believed with less.
Behind every dream there is always someone
Yearning for love and the thrill of success.

I'm only waiting for you, like you'd wait for me,
Perhaps only more intently, I'm sure you'd agree.
Time and tide, reality hanging on every word,
I'm not wasting my time—that would be absurd.

Otis Saturday died in 2010, but that was then,
When I possibly might have cared, but I don't.
He was one of many gifted, yet unknown men,
Who hung like a doll from a rope, but I won't.

The Employment of Freddy and Ralph

Freddy and Ralph were the very best of pals
Who worked together and I guess they always shall.
They each held a job answering the doors uptown
In a sprawling mansion of a rich man's town.

While they were drinking, attending their chores,
A series of rapping came upon the front doors.
Said Freddy, "I'll get the door, since I heard it first,
And I'll be quick, lest the rapping get worse!"

Yet together they ran like bats out of hell,
When suddenly someone rang the backdoor bell.
Said Ralph, "Now there are two doors for us to receive –
You get the back; I'll get the front before they leave."

So, Freddy turned around, and as he went, he cursed,
Because it was him who heard the front door first.
Along the way, he began to feel a little bit sad,
Whilst remembering all the better jobs he once had.

Then in his frustration, he was overwhelmed and cried
As he put a hand over his heart, then fell down and died.
So, in the bitter end, Ralph answered his call,
But poor Freddy succumbed to the alcohol.

In our lives, there are jobs that we must do,
And someone will always have a nicer job than you.
Perhaps we should not pay attention to envy or doubt,
For its why we're employed, and not what about.

The Laziness of William Tooley

"Too much work ruins the body,"
I always heard William Tooley say.
He'd smoke a cigar and drink his ale
While watching TV throughout the day.

He had a meal just every so often
And only if he could roll out of bed,
For if he were more tired than hungry,
He'd rather sleep some more instead.

Sometimes he'd arise in the morning
At exactly six o'clock—rain or shine—
To steal someone's milk so that he could
Slip back into bed just before nine.

By noon, he would go into town
To cop a cola from the soda jerk.
When asked why he wasn't working,
He'd say, "Hey, it's too hot to work."

He'd use the diner's bathroom
When he had need to relieve his bladder,
And because he never washed his hands,
This made the owner even madder.

"Hey Tooley, where I come from,
We wash our hands after we pee!"
"So, learn not to pee on your hands,"
William would reply gleefully.

Although he was a dreadful sight,
I couldn't help but feel sorry for him.
A man of the world with tattoos
On every skinny, wrinkled limb.

He was the last to enter the church
Long after the services began.
And during the sermon, he'd fall asleep
If he was bored or didn't understand.

Yet somehow, he always woke up
When it was time for the feast,
And he was the first one in line
To shake hands with the priest.

Instead of working a job to survive,
He lived long without occupation,
And whilst others carried the load,
He enjoyed a life-long vacation.

The Loathing For Simon Sullivan

Simon Sullivan is a miserly man,
Who lives for money and keeps all he can.
When his granny died at age ninety-four,
He uttered a cry and then fell to the floor.
It wasn't from grief that he could not bear it,
But from all the money he would soon inherit.

He doesn't give money to the poor or dying,
He just saves it all without even trying.
He's forty years old and still lives at home,
And still expects his mother to pay back her loan.
She washes his clothes and feeds him still,
Even though he wrote her out of his will.

Wretched, vile Simon—how I loathe him so,
I despise him from his wig to the gout in his toe.
I've found nothing good, and I've looked very hard,
Why should he care with money buried in the yard?
He even gets everything for free and I know why –
He has a family that knows how to multiply.

His brother's a dentist and gets checkups for free,
His nephew's a priest—even gets eternity!
His uncle tunes his car because he's a mechanic,
His sister, the nurse, gives him pills so he won't panic.
His daughter's a maid and his brother his dresser
And all they can say is, "Yes Sir, no Sir, yes Sir."

He sleeps on the job when he isn't daydreaming,
And lies to his employees when he isn't screaming.
He's the most unhappy man that I've ever met,
But he could care less because all his money is net.
He believes he is well-liked, but I do not know why,
With what he pays for help, they can barely scrape by.

He will bore you to tears just standing there,
As he turns green with envy if you have more hair.
It's amazing to me how much money he rakes in;
He amasses so much; I must believe it's a sin.
How I loathe Simon Sullivan—how I wait for the day
When someone takes all of his money way.

The Plumbing of Tolliver Hayes

Tolliver Hayes was a plumber who plumbed day and night
As long as every building in town was fitted with pipe.
He was on call—to fix leaks and keep everything tight,
And he made a decent living, so why should he gripe?

He was getting close to retirement after 45 years,
And it wouldn't be long before he hung up his belt.
It was his own plumbing that sometimes-brought tears
From a lump in his groin that he often times felt.

When pipes get old in both our homes and our bodies,
Repair will be needed to keep everything working.
With age comes weakening bones and antibodies
And replacement parts to keep old pipes from jerking.

The Town Drunk

Sit down young lad, I have a story to tell
Of a Twin Mountain man whom many knew well.
I cannot disclose his name, for he went by none,
Except for the curses used by everyone.

He lived in a hut made of canvas and rag,
And drank all his meals from a paper bag.
He owned a dog that went everywhere with him,
His name was Timothy, but he just called him 'Tim'.

He covered his bald head with a Yankees cap
That he stole from another bum taking a nap.
His boots are well-worn and his coat is in tatters;
A walking clothesline if any of this matters.

He possessed a corn pipe and a hunting knife,
And I think he had a son by a wandering wife,
But of all his treasures, of which he had few,
He prized most of all his still and his brew.

He would walk into town a few times a year
To peddle his whiskey and his version of beer.
With the sale of a few bottles, he'll never know wealth,
But at least he is happy and still has his health.

The Sleeplessness of George

George, a man unbeknownst to many,
Was rich once, but now without a penny.
One night he simply could not fall asleep,
And then the nights turned into a week.

He tried every remedy known to man,
But never would his eyes fill with sand.
He counted sheep 'til he could count no more,
And would have sold his soul for a single snore.

Then upon one restless and stormy night,
He heard a voice and turned on the light.
Before him stood the Sandman, he guessed,
And said, "Please Sir, I too need some rest."

So, with one wave of his shadowy hand,
He filled George's eyes with enchanted sand.
He slept for days and dreamt many dreams,
And alas he was content, or so it seems . . .

The Birthdays of Lester Fothergill

It was birthdays Lester Fothergill hated,
Any and all birthdays—on time or belated.
As a child, he always detested the toys,
The parties, and all of that birthday noise.

Long ago, he stopped remembering the date
Of blowing out candles on a birthday cake.
How he despised receiving those birthday gifts,
Getting slapped on the back with a birthday kiss.

He loathes birthday parties and celebration.
I think he'd have more fun under sedation.
He hates counting the days and losing sleep
And all those presents he's expected to keep.

Though I am sure that he would never make mention
I know that he enjoys all of the attention.
I suppose it's a wonder he survived all sixty-four,
But I'm certain he'll love to hate many more.

My Friend, Brian

One day, a dear friend of mine, named Brian,
Appeared at my door with something on his mind,
But he couldn't remember no matter how hard he tried
So, he sat down at my feet and then he cried.

"For crying out loud, Brian," I screamed,
"Just look at what you're doing—making a scene.
You're beginning to embarrass me before my neighbors
What's wrong with you, and why this fit of the vapors?

"I can see it all know, all in black and white:
'Man cries at friend's doorstep all day and night . . .'
What are you trying to do, Brian—ruin my career?
Stop all of this crying and get up off your rear!

"Don't do this to me again, don't do this at all –
You know how upset I get whenever you bawl.
If you don't stop it now, I'll have you taken away
And see to it that the key gets thrown far away!"

A moment later, after such harsh words were spoken,
Up stood my friend Brian, completely soakin'.
He still couldn't remember what set him off cryin',
And this was the last I saw of my friend, Brian.

An Ode for the Porcelain Throne

Sit down, my friend, and rest your weary frame.
Do what you must and do it without shame.
This little throne your fanny occupies,
Makes all men equal beneath the skies.
The King, the Queen, the wiseman and the fool,
Take down their pants to sit on this stool.
The millionaire who dwells in marble halls,
Ain't better than me when nature calls.
Even the Pope with his satin underwear,
Cannot keep from exposing his derrière.
A poor man's gruel and a rich man's food, by heck—
When they get there, are running neck and neck.
With enough magazines and books to read,
Don't take too much time with others in need,
And one more thought I leave with you my friend,
Don't waste all the paper on your big rear end.

Bloody Bones, the Ogre

Bloody Bones the ogre was a very foul foe,
Who was meaner than mean, as most fiends go.
He was covered with hair from his head to his toe,
And folks suffered every evil this monster could sow.

It was difficult for anyone who believed,
How such a creature could have been conceived.
Never for a moment was his anger relieved—
It was from the devil his wrath was received.

Every Spring and Autumn, he'd make his quest
To fill his belly with a damsel in distress.
He'd storm every castle from the east to the west
And from the north to the south before he would rest.

Brad the Good came into town without a cent,
And learned if he would fight, he'd be free of rent,
So, he sharpened his sword and set up his tent
And after this ogre—on his way he went.

After a day and a half of looking wide and far,
He stopped off for a whiskey at a local bar.
When quenched of his thirst, he found the north star,
And on his way, he was, on this quest so bizarre.

Under the full moon on the second night,
Brad looked to his left and then he looked to his right.
He saw Bloody Bones the ogre, and so began the fight,
And Brad fought this ogre with all of his might.

Bloody Bones the ogre had not been well fed,
Nor had he the time to get rest in his bed.
So, with one great stroke, Brad chopped off his head
Leaving the beast in its blood on the ground for dead.

The moral of this story—a forgotten one, I might add—
Not every champion has a name that's big, bold and bad.
I suppose it's not a great name, like this story's had,
But you cannot judge a man's strength, even if it is Brad.

A Hanging

Across the streets of cobblestone,
From inside the belly of my father's coach,
The news of a hanging must get home,
Lest I be scolded, and with much reproach.

"Today, a hanging in the village square!"
The crier shouted, with a voice of woe,
"All ye of weakest frame beware,
For the devil himself comes for her soul!"

A woman of the street arrived there first—
To give her penny for the printed news,
And as an infant on her withered breast nursed,
Her children looked on, somewhat confused.

Toothless grins of glee, and eyes wide with wonder,
Spread across otherwise empty faces.
The distance carried the dull groans of thunder
As the peasant farmers each took their places.

Clowns and jugglers appeared on the scene,
Amusing the crowds as they gathered still.
I awaited the arrival of this wretched fiend,
Shackled in the death cart from over the hill.

With the loud arrival of the prison carts,
We doubted the evidence of our own eyes.
We looked at each other like drunken tarts,
For this hanging was a murder in disguise!

The death cart rocked along before us,
Carrying a girl—seventeen or less.
We crossed our hearts, and cried, "Oh Jesus,
Certainly, this hanging is only a jest."

My heart pumped blood to my ashen face,
As they slung the rope around her throat.
Then the executioner relaxed the pace,
When from a pocket he produced a note.

"Hear ye, hear ye, all who gather—hear!
Ye are to witness the slaying of a witch!
No longer will we live in trouble and fear,
Once I pull on this lever of pine and pitch!"

With a violent motion, her young body shook,
Then the crowd applauded and cheered,
But little did they know, as they passively stood,
There was much to worry about and to be feared.

We no longer hang young women as witches,
Worse than this we give them the rope.
Today we place our faith in all of the riches
That we can stuff into a Church's envelope.

The Ghost of Til-Gaviel

Nearing the hamlet of Til-Gaviel
On a night ago three centuries,
An agent of the underworld appeared
On the cliffs weathering hammering seas.

From the direction of the Strath Gap,
A cleft in the cliffs that still stand,
Seen by shepherds around a fire,
Emerged a headless, legless man.

In a skirted garment and a pistol in his belt
Of then a sea-faring smuggler of tea,
He passed by the men rolling side to side
In the manner of walking a deck at sea.

Its neck glistened in the bright moonlight,
Its head lolling between its shoulder blades.
Passing by the men in the campfire light,
Of the seven, only two shepherds stayed.

In its arms it carried a heavy sack,
With his long pigtail trailing the ground.
For an hour the two men followed,
Not knowing where the ghost was bound.

In Til-Gaviel, it stopped by the well,
Its head swinging against its back.
Bending over as if to see,
Into the hole it heaved the sack.

It climbed up over the stone well
And then threw itself into the hole,
And as if the ghost were still a corpse,
A splash was heard from the water below.

The two men remained until the sun rose high,
And went through the town sharing their tale,
But no man dared to venture down
To retrieve the treasure, lest they fail.

Then out of the crowd that gathered still,
A man came forward who would make the quest.
He'd go down into the well with a lamp
To seek what kept this spirit from rest.

From a windlass winched down to gloom
He traversed the cold walls of the narrow hole.
Just as the lantern light began to go out
He fished through the water with his pole.

At last! A gray bundle seen half-submerged,
Was pulled out of the well for all to see.
The crowd pressed closer to the canvas sack
The kind of bag used to transport Black tea.

The carnival air of the crowd dispersed
When the satchel released a horrid stench:
Two legs still shod in leather boots
With white bones protruding from rotting flesh.

Even the lad refused to venture further
Until a fisherman stepped out from the crowd.
Faces rimmed the tiny opening from above –
As many as the opening of the well allowed.

With screams echoing from the depth below,
The men pulled on the rope down the well.
As they strained to haul up the dripping mass,
The crowd stood back, forewarned of the smell.

As the fisherman opened the bag with his knife,
The crowd stood back from what was within:
A skull exposed through decaying flesh
Joined to a trunk by a mere flap of skin.

Surmised to be a smuggler from sheltered coves,
A shipper of silk, tobacco, and tea,
His witnesses guessed his throat was slit
Then his body hacked to hide in the sea.

The ghost of Til-Gaviel walked no more,
Once a man of the living from where it came.
No desire to torment, but to communicate
A burial for the corpse from which it sprang.

The Epitaphs of Alfie Baker and Stanley Cook

Down the road a piece there is a cabin
Tucked under tall trees of pine and oak.
In the yard an axe lays on the ground,
Its blade bloodied and the handle broke.
Inside, a clock ticks away in silence,
Its chains rattling against the glass.
A leaf drifts down from the sky above
And dies on the axe out on the grass.

The Trees

There once was a time, claimed Celtic bards,
When all trees forever remained green,
From the darkest forests to common yards,
And all of the gardens in between.

Even in the harshest ice and snow,
Not one single leaf turned brown,
To flutter upon the winds that blow
And fall to its death upon the ground.

In those days, every tree had a soul
And waved their limbs proudly in the air.
In every meadow, pasture, and knoll
Not one tree in the forests stood bare.

Late one September, when it becomes cold,
A flock of redwings halted their flight
To rest on branches so lofty and old,
Before their migration into the night.

On the next morning, as the sun arose,
One such redwing remained behind.
With a broken wing, it was disposed
To find shelter among the oaks and pine.

Leaping and fluttering from tree to tree,
Seeking shelter from the rain and cold,
None of the wood gave sanctuary
To permit this wounded bird to take hold.

The birch and the oak swayed in the wind
Taking no heed of the bird's request.
Even the sad willow kept it pinned
From using her mournful twigs for a nest.

Searching from below and looking high,
The bird discovered a spruce, fir, and pine.
She hopped and flapped up into the sky,
Branch by branch along the tree line.

At last, the bird reached the tallest spruce,
Which warmly received her just in time.
The scotch pine offered its needles for use
To shelter the redwing in its natural twine.

The fir tree hid her from a great height
Shielding her from the morning sun's rays.
Even the juniper, with its berries now ripe,
Fed the bird until it would see better days.

For the trees that showed no mercy or aid,
Now when the winds blow at the first frost,
The green in their leaves will begin to fade
And fall down to the ground, forever lost.

In Memory of Cora and Walter Bean

Cora and Walter Bean were both eighty years of age,
Getting ready to rest in their eternal graves.
They lived in a shack that some might call a house,
With a mule, a dog, a cat—and even a mouse.
All their lives, they scrimped, scratched, and saved
For a home in the town on a road that was paved.
They fancied a farm of pears, plums, and avocado's
Yet in spite of their dreams, poverty always followed.

Though hard labor plowed their backs over time,
Not once did they cheat a neighbor, or resort to crime.
There are those who have made some bad choices,
Even when it was a life guided by voices.
Is it not from who you know, and by whom you're bred,
That these folks can count the blessings upon their head?
Is it because such kin feel entitled to curse
Folks like Cora and Walter, making their lives worse?

"You go around once," we say, and most believe it,
But what of the unfortunate—their fields are unweeded.
The Lord gives freely, and He freely takes away
To give into the hands that fold at night to pray.
With all of their wealth, that crowd can't imagine why,
Their anxiety and boredom reach out to the sky.
If they'd seek for the comfort of a contented heart,
Then perhaps, they'd see the suffering, and do their part.

Our Lord spoke of a man who buried his money away,
And now that man endures the sting of eternal dismay,
But to the generous—as the Lord most certainly was—
Surely, it's these whom He blesses, and these He loves.
The demise of Cora and Walter will remain with us still,
But so will the parched papers of a dead man's will.
With the passage of time, all of us too will pass,
So, let's make good memories, which are meant to last.

The Court Jester

The courts of Palace gold, in days of old,
Echoed waves of laughter throughout its halls.
Every king who enjoyed a good laugh,
Engaged a jester, a juggler of balls.

Each evening after a long day of toil,
The court shouted and cheered for the jester.
He would lighten all their sorrow and pain
Before misery had a chance to fester.

They heaped flowers at his stocking feet
When he danced on the floor of Persian tile.
They hailed the king with eyes of wonder
Whenever the jester made their faces smile.

Then one day, after many years had passed,
The old feet that once danced on the floor,
Were no longer covered with fragrant petals,
Because the jokes were not funny anymore.

Yet no matter how hard he tried,
The crowd would listen, but not be moved.
He'd dance and juggle and joke some more,
But still they yawned and unapproved.

To save face, the king banished the jester
From entertaining in his court,
And more years passed without a laugh
Until the tempers were running short.

One day, when the king needed a laugh,
The court jester was nowhere to be found.
The king's guards had to search high and low
Before they found him lying on the ground.

Come, you peasant swine, up on your feet,
You are needed by His Majesty, the King.
Get yourself dressed and gather your balls,
Then proceed to the court to do your thing.

The guards helped him stand on his feet,
Just to knock him down with a curse.
They mocked him as they delivered blows
Among his desperate pleas for a nurse.

Before the court he stood in filth,
His battered cheek glistening with blood.
Before His Majesty and the court,
He stood dejected, covered with mud.

When he finally opened his mouth to speak,
He drew a breath, but it was his very last.
Then as he crumbled to the tiled floor,
How the king and the court laughed and laughed.

The Beast Beneath My Bed

After my folks laid me down to bed,
From beneath it, a sense of dread.
As the last beams of light
Turned into blackest night,
I lay in anticipation –
My life hanging by a thread.

Out though my window,
Where I might dare to peep,
I fear the apparitions
That I perceive in my sleep.
Shadowy figures out on the lawn
Keep me in terror until the dawn.

Throughout the night,
As I cover my head,
The beast's appetite
Shakes my bed.
It raves all through the night—
Until the new morning light.

In the evenings, as I grew older,
I become less afraid, perhaps bolder.
The beast that lives beneath my bed
Was me all along, inside my head.
As a child, there came an end to the beast,
But now as a man, the horror's increased.

The Ballad of Molly and Dale

Molly and Dale were two good friends,
Who liked to watch the roosters and hens.
They'd laugh and laugh and laugh and laugh,
Until their sides felt like they'd break in half.

Then one day, Dale had an idea or two,
And told Molly that he had something to do.
So, he went to the store, and bought a bed,
And set in by the fence, to fall on it instead.

"This way," said Dale to Molly, "if we should laugh,
We'll have a soft place to land to break in half.
We're bruised, battered, bloodied and torn—
And besides, the rocks and stones are getting worn."

So, they watched and laughed, watched, and laughed,
And bounced on the bed until their sides split in half,
But along came her father, a man of the world and proud,
And he spoke to them with a voice—angry and loud.

"What is this scene for my eyes on thee to fall,
That I see my girl and a man in bed with alcohol?
With my shotgun, shall the both of you be wed,
Before either one of you bounce off of that there bed!"

So, within the hour, they were man and wife,
And began their journey in the married life,
But before you knew it, the years flew by,
And it wasn't long before Molly and Dale died.

The moral of this story, the moral of this tale,
Is to be sure what you buy on a mattress sale.
Beds of all kinds—especially ones in which we awaken,
Can deceive you into a course of life, much forsaken.

The Insatiable Hunger of Jethro Hapgood

Each night when Jethro Hapgood returned to his home,
No messages were left for him on his telephone,
So, in sadness, he would go to his kitchen icebox
And unlock the door he fitted with a dozen locks.

As much as he protected his food from the bears,
(He lived in a small cabin, if anyone cares)
They'd break into his home when he was out—
Hunting for squirrels and fishing for trout.

With his chin lower than a pigs on slaughter day,
And with nothing to eat, he just walked away.
"How long can this last? My body is wasted.
I'd sell my soul for food that can be tasted."

So, with nothing to eat, back outside he went
Like a ravenous dog still out on the scent.
After a while, he ran into a man,
Down at the crossroads, eating beans from a can.

"You look like a man that could use a good meal,"
Said the man, mixing the beans—"how about a deal?"
"I have no money, as all of it has been spent,
But in exchange, you can live with me, free of rent."

"I have a place to live; it's not money I'm after,"
The man with the beans said, crying with laughter.
"But if it's the food you desire from my bowl,
Why don't you consider selling me your soul?"

"Will it be painful if you take my soul from me?"
Asked Jethro Hapgood, as he got down on a knee.
"You won't feel a thing, I can promise you that.
I'll give you enough food to make you big and fat!"

So, Jethro sold his soul for all the beans he could eat—
He exchanged his soul, which he deemed obsolete.
He returned to his cabin with a loaded backpack,
And died seven months later from a heart attack.

Alice Thatcher

Alice Thatcher had the prettiest face from all around,
And lived in a house by a lake in my hometown.
When we were kids, we skinny-dipped in summer eves,
And in the autumn, we played for hours in the leaves.

We held hands bringing smiles to elderly faces,
And had many adventures in hidden places.
We laughed through our noses when the pastor prayed
And stayed out after dark when we often played.

As we grew older, we somehow began to drift,
And no longer did I receive a birthday or Christmas gift.
Into our teens as we left our childhood behind,
I longed for her touch, but she had other things in mind.

One day I will never forget, as I was on my way home,
Kicking stones out of the road while walking alone,
I caught a glimpse of her beside a barn in the grass,
Moving with a boy who was popular in my class.

I wept in our hidden places by the shimmering lake,
And since that day, I've struggled with such heartache,
Until I learned many years later that she lived in the city
Where she earned a living with that face so pretty.

The Village Idiot

Bowser Wright was the result of when cousins unite,
You could tell by the way he looked you in the eye.
He was dim-witted and he just didn't seem right—
He wandered the streets without really knowing why.

He had a cough that made people laugh when they heard it
And he walked like the seat of his pants were always full.
His canned-heat stew wasn't that bad when he stirred it—
Never enough to fill his belly, but a good mouthful.

He'd rarely look at anyone in the eye—thank God for that.
He never begged for food but was somehow always fat.
At times you'd hear him laughing or perhaps it was a cry;
You could not really tell unless you asked him why.

Every village is certain to have its customary fool,
But as idiots go, our hamlet was surely blessed,
For not only did he ever attend a proper school,
But whatever he learned, I'm sure he only guessed.

It's not that I despised him—he seemed nice enough—
A community member away from the big city,
Pushing his market basket loaded with the stuff
That might make one feel sad, perhaps even pity.

I suppose it's a blessing for us to have our own clown
Not every village has one, not every town . . .
But he's one of our own and ours to adore,
A reprieve from the lashings we save for the poor.

The Phantoms of Bulwark Castle

Somewhere deep within these castle walls,
Some say they can hear voices and whispers.
Centuries of sadness consumes empty spaces,
Through all of the summers and the winters.

A few have seen two boys holding hands
Walking the endless halls by candlelight.
I suppose it isn't hard to understand
How two phantoms can create such fright.

They were banished to an unused room
By their mother, the Duchess, for a petty crime.
A punishment for a single act of mischief
To contemplate their actions until dinnertime.

After hours of entertaining their guests,
The Duke and Duchess ascended the steps.
Huddling for warmth as they entered the room,
They beheld the horror of when one forgets.

In a corner lay the two lads embraced,
Frozen together as they tried to keep warm.
Tears of ice smeared their bluish lips,
As they might have wished they were never born.

As the light flickered from the burning wick,
Illuminating the vapors of their heated breath,
They approached the bodies of their frozen sons,
And into glassy eyes they gazed at death.

Removing loose blocks of the castle wall,
They worked against time without making a noise.
In the secret tomb they said their goodbyes,
And in anguished haste they buried the boys.

No one ever found a trace of the little lads
After days of searching each passageway,
And forever within the castle's crumbling walls,
Roam the little phantoms to this very day.

The Retirement of Malcolm McCready

Malcolm McCready is a quiet and peaceful man,
Who lives on a pension the best way he can.
Not much of a talker—I expect he never was—
He's not known for what he says, but for what he does.

He lights the streets for travelers every night
By lighting the wicks of the lamp posts bright.
Up his sturdy ladder, he lights up every lamp,
Then closes the glass against the night so damp.

Into his hands he blows heated breath,
While in between lightings, he takes a rest.
Into the mist he blows smoke from his pipe
And chews on an apple, though it still isn't ripe.

With everyone sleeping upon beds of feather,
Malcolm makes his rounds in unpleasant weather.
He looks forward to his home, which gives it heat
So that he can take off his boots and thaw his feet.

In a time when our youth abhors the old,
They forsake the wisdom only the aged can hold.
For all the experience he gained through the years,
Malcolm is the future every young man fears.

As the young continue to walk by the light of day,
His evening lamps keep them from losing their way.
Should they seek the wisdom they seem to implore,
They'd find great wealth from this man they ignore.

The Bride of Halliwell Hall

Gaelic halls bear the laughter of wedded bliss,
But never greater than the Hall of Halliwell.
The day that shines brighter in most of our lives
Is marked in our memories by a wedding bell.

Near Aberdeenshire, there is a spectral bride
That haunts the crumbing walls of porous stone.
Throughout the corridors of faded tapestry
The shadows in the corners are her only home.

It's been many long years since laughter
Echoed throughout the cold, isolated peak,
When the disappearance of the Halliwell bride
Curtailed a lively game of hide and seek.

A simple child's game was all she asked
Of her family, the guests, and the groom,
And in all the gaiety, no one suspected
That this enjoyable lark would lead to doom.

She searched for the perfect hiding place
Where she could cleverly hide herself,
But after hours of their laborious search,
Everyone shared what the bridegroom felt.

It had become dark, and all was in disarray
As the family continued the frantic search.
The groom sent servants to His Majesty
And to the Bishop praying in his church.

Hours turned to days, and days into weeks,
But still the bride could not be found.
Some thought she fell into the river from a window
Where she certainly would have drowned.

Others whispered that she left with another
After stealing the groom's silver and gold,
But we all know quite differently now
Since this tale has been often told.

Whatever the rumors, they all came to an end
When the bridegroom's bullet suicidal came.
Thereafter, the great doors of iron and wood
Were locked tight within the Hall's forsaken name.

Years later with a shriek and then the screaming,
The mystery of the great hall came to an end
When a curious servant explored the attic,
And found a chest that he opened once again.

Inside lay human bones among the bridal finery
Of a wedding which took place so long ago.
Indeed, she had found the perfect place to hide,
But as the lid crashed down, she was trapped below.

CRIMES

Dio

The orange glowing remnant of the day retreated from the horizon as the array of stars began to appear through the heavy black sky of night. Among a thicket of palm trees, a hunched over figure chopped the last grisly fragment from the badly mutilated body. In the shallow hole next to the dismembered thing, lay segments of what might have been human. He was not certain, nor did he care.

When he finished hacking the body into unrecognizable pieces, he tossed the ax aside in disgust. His lower back ached, and his eyes squinted in pain as he stooped to pick up a shovel. He took notice of his vile handiwork as he grasped the long wooden handle with his calloused hands. His body jerked sharply as he thrust the spade into the pile of dark damp earth, and his hands throbbed painfully with each shovel-full as he quickly covered every trace of the wretched evidence.

There was no reasonable explanation for the ominous duty he conducted with such mechanical precision. He was not even aware that it was a pretentious act of genetic manipulation, which placed him at this desolate place; in this dreary hour; in this dreadful predicament. With the blood and fluids of the corpse seeping into the loose soil beneath it, he felt no remorse, no regret. Had the authorities discovered him burying the thing in his frenzied labor, he would have had no account, no rationalization for his actions.

Beads of sweat dribbled down his unshaven face as they traced his pursed, thin lips. He collected the salty perspiration with his tongue and spat into the hole with a sneer of loathing. The thing could not be identified as human. What would he be charged with anyway?

By the time the sun disappeared with the onset of the evening's humid haze, the macabre job was finished. He plucked his handkerchief from his back pocket and wiped away the perspiration from the back of his neck and his dirty face. The hard, wrinkled cloth reeked, and the offensive stench stung his nose. The night sky was overwhelmingly heavy; he could feel the darkness enclosing him like a blanket. The stifling silence was eerily broken with the flick of his flashlight. He heard absolutely nothing, but somehow sensed he was not alone. With a sniff, he thrust his dirty handkerchief deep into his back pocket, and picking up his tools, he slung them over his shoulder. As he walked away, he peered back to get one last look of the freshly disturbed soil of the ghastly grave. The wet earth sparkled in the beam of his flashlight. With each short stride he made away from the morbid place, his footsteps resonated off the swampy, flat, moist surface with a swishing noise. He began to whistle to lighten his mood.

Past the long, fluttering leaves dangling from gently swaying palm trees, he heard an agonizing, wailing scream in the distance. The screams echoed in shrilling intervals until drifting away into silence, only to return in louder outbursts with each contraction of its monstrous diaphragm.

The gravedigger quickened his step as he trudged his way through the mire. Excitement from fear and curiosity pounded in his chest, yet he instinctively knew there was safety in the distance between himself and the distant source of the tortured cries.

The unmarked and defiled grave site was now shrouded in complete darkness. Yet, the unholy burial was not entirely unattended. Something tall and malevolent, and indescribably inhuman stood beside it. It towered over the swampy mound of earth, leaves, and sticks, gazing upon it with moist, red eyes bewildered in disbelief. It could almost taste the blood in its throat, fueled by the pounding of its massive heart. It looked to the west and saw the dim speck of light gradually disappear out of sight. It snapped its gaze back to the unhallowed pile of disturbed soil, longing for what lay in pieces beneath the mud, but not knowing how to reach it.

It felt the dull spirit of loneliness invade its senses. In frustration it could not identify the churning pain it felt in its belly, forcing it to its knees. It ran its fingers through the mound, delicately at first so as to not disturb the matted pile of muck and vegetation, and then more violently, whimpering, like a bewildered child lost in the forest begging to be found. The quiet moans gained momentum as exasperation set in, and once again, it cried out in a battery of furious roars of rage. It buried its chest into the cool, soft mud, and then rolled onto its back, screaming out its rage in scream after anguished scream; its extremities high in the air; slippery mud oozing through its clenched fists against the luminous moon bearing down unsympathetically. It rolled over and over in the muck like a crocodile devouring its prey; its mind overwhelmed by grief and lost in misery.

Soon the breeze became a wind, and the moon became obscured by feathery clouds encircling it like giant ghostly fingers reaching for a doorknob, an escape from this pitiable scene on earth far below.

And then it rained.

Keith stood before a ceiling-to-floor window and watched the cars drive by through the deep puddles forming in the street from a sudden torrential downpour. He folded his arms and turned around to view the warmly lit auditorium of the tiny New Hampshire University. With a three-day beard, unkempt hair, and in his worn-out Khaki cargo shorts and green and white rugby shirt, he did not look much like an anthropologist to the students he had just given a lecture to.

His wife, Janis, a geneticist, was wrapping up her own lecture on hereditary-related birth defects for an introductory genetics class. Six months ago, they were married in Firth, Scotland, where she grew up. After their honeymoon, he decided to take three months off to draft a book about Scottish history and his most recent research as an anthropologist in northern Scotland after graduating from the University of St. Andrews.

Only twenty-four, his wife appeared more like a college student herself. Very attractive with a youthful complexion, she had no trouble getting the attention from a crowd—especially the men. She wanted the audience of mostly men to give their attention to her lecture more than to her appearance, so she wore a baggy turtleneck sweater hung fashionably from her narrow shoulders and a plaid skirt to help hide her voluptuous figure. Her pixie-round face was fair and translucent as porcelain, accented by pouting red lips and clear, green eyes beneath high arching eyebrows. She didn't use makeup and wore very little jewelry aside from her wedding and engagement rings, and she liked to wear white dock sneakers without socks. Indeed, Janis was a beautiful woman and Keith considered himself a fortunate man, indeed.

Already an hour into her lecture, she stood casually in front of her audience, commanding attention with an economy of hand gestures and a musical-sounding Scottish accent. She spoke authoritatively with an economic vocabulary in an effort to keep her audience from sleeping.

"Though individual genetic disorders are rare," she said, readjusting the slipping microphone stand, "collectively, they comprise over 15,000 recognized genetic disorders. Three to five percent of all infant deaths result in congenital malformations; 20 to 30 percent of all infant deaths being attributed to genetic disorders. Birth weight-specific infant mortality rates can be attributed to congenital abnormalities."

She glanced over to her husband leaning against the enormous window off to the right side of the stage and shared a smile with him. He winked back, and nodded downward toward his wristwatch, indicating that her time was almost up.

"Additionally," she continued, the corners of her smile falling gracefully, "30 to 50 percent of post-neonatal deaths are due to congenital malformations. No less than 50% of intellectual disabilities has a genetic basis, and sadly, 15 percent of all cancers have an inherited susceptibility.

"As you all are aware, genetics is the branch of biology concerned with heredity and individual characteristics. Specific conditions and rare disorders may have a genetic basis. Where this is the case, there will be a variety of causes. For example, the causes may include a single abnormal gene, a chromosomal abnormality, or a genetic predisposition allied to other factors.

"A mutant, that is, an abnormal gene is one where a gene may be considered a variant of a so-called, normal gene. This change may occur spontaneously by chance and have no significance for the individual concerned. In other cases, the gene, which mutates, thereby changing its character, may give rise to specific inherited disorders where there is no previous family history. Such a gene, in specific circumstances determined by status, can cause a specific disorder. Inheritance may be autosomal dominant, autosomal recessive or X-linked recessive.

"There are a number of techniques that are used to diagnose pre-natal defects in fetuses whose mothers are at risk of having a baby with an abnormality, such as an amniocentesis, chorionic villus sampling, a fetoscopy, or ultrasound scanning. There may be a question of a family history of an anomaly, or that the parents have already had one child with, say, a heart defect. On the other hand, pre-natal testing may be performed on the grounds of the age of the mother."

Keith tapped the face of his wristwatch with a finger, looking over the rims of his round glasses, signaling her to bring her lecture to a close. They had three hours to get to Logan Airport for a trip to the 10,000 Islands northwest of the Florida Everglades.

"Well, I'm afraid I'm out of time, everyone," she informed the audience, which spawned a thunderous clapping of applause.

"My husband is signaling me that we need to leave." The applauding suddenly shifted to a chaotic chorus of light-hearted booing and foot-stamping.

"Alright, everyone," the Dean of the college interrupted, taking the stage with a wave. "If anyone is interested in Dr. Brannigan's book, we have copies procured by the college, and are available to you in the hallway in front of the bookstore. If you give her a moment," he said darting a wink in her direction, "I'll bet she'll sign a few copies on her way out."

"Great," Keith sighed to himself, snatching a large satchel. On the way to collect his wife through the crowd, the Dean and several students intercepted his wife.

"You gave an excellent presentation, Dr. Brannigan," he assured her, shaking her delicate hand.

"I can't thank you enough for coming to us on such short notice. I only wish we had more time so that I could bring you home for dinner. My wife makes a killer martini, and her shrimp scampi isn't that bad."

They shared a laugh.

Turning his attention to Keith, who by now was walking toward the podium, the Dean said, "I understand you two are now leaving for your vacation all the way down in the everglades?"

"Pretty much right," Keith replied. "We've been invited to spend a few days with Dr. Valter Belski at his home on one of the islands."

"I believe his work led to the growing of ears on mice, or something extraordinary, like that," the Dean said, "and he lives on his own island . . . "

"I believe he owns several of them actually," Janis interjected, fishing through her purse for a pen.

"Must be nice," the Dean said, helping them cut a path through the crowd to the front doors, "but I thought he passed away sometime in the mid 2000's."

"Only from professional society," Keith said with a smile, "I'm sure he's still trying to figure out what else he can grow on the backs of mice."

"Interesting . . . " the dean responded, slipping Janis an envelope with a check in it for their lectures.

She signed books for about ten minutes before Keith urgently rushed her out the door, through the pelting rain, and to their rented car. Two hours later, they arrived at Logan Airport for what he hoped would be an uneventful trip. He could not have underestimated it any more.

Boarding the plane at 6:30 that evening, they were eager for a quiet visit to a peaceful island in the middle of nowhere. They slept on the way, and landed in Sarasota, Florida around 11:00 PM. From there, they took a quick hop in a charted Cessna to Titan Island, thirty-five miles southwest of Long Boat Key.

They disembarked from the small plane and headed for the gate for a pre-arranged meeting with a "short, middle-aged, dark-skinned man" holding a placard with the name, "Brannigan." Within minutes, they located him, perfectly matching the description provided by Belski over the telephone the day before. Keith offered to shake his hand, but it was not reciprocated. In a cantankerous tone, the diminutive man instructed them to follow him, and they quietly obliged. Within minutes, they ended up at a 1976 white Cadillac limousine. The man ostentatiously opened a door for them, and taking their luggage, he proceeded to the back of the limo. The time it took him to get around to closing the trunk seemed long enough for Keith to check his watch.

"What's he doing back there?" he impatiently asked his wife.

"Relax, honey," she said, "he's probably arranging it all to fit . . . "

"What, around a dead body?"

"Relax, will ya?" she smiled, "let's just enjoy the ride. It's late and he's probably just as tired as we are." She slid into his side as he slung his arm around her, drawing her close.

When the driver finally took his seat and closed the door, he started the limo and told them it was only a short ride to the boat.

"The boat . . . " Janis whispered. "I forgot about the boat ride . . . "

"Not to worry, sweet thing," Keith whispered back into her ear. "We'll sleep in tomorrow . . . I'll buy you breakfast. My treat."

"Sounds pretty nice," Janis said, closing her eyes.

Once they reached the solitary dock at the end of a long, serpentine dirt road—much of it still in disrepair from the merciless hurricane the year before—all three figures emptied out of the car.

"I will get your things," the driver announced in a Haitian accent.

While Janis and Keith patiently waited for him to return from the back of the car with their luggage, they saw the boat that would bring them to their destination. It was an elegant looking craft, a 45-footer, Keith surmised.

"Crickey," Keith gushed, in his Australian accent.

"What's the matter, honey?" Janis asked him.

"The Dean gave us a check for only sixty bucks!"

Janis looked into the open envelope in Keith's hands and shook her head in disbelief.

"That's what we get for agreeing to 'lecture by donation,'" Janis sighed, disappointed, "but at least the school purchased a few dozen copies of my book."

"Yeah, but sixty bucks? That is such an insult. Guess we should have taken him up on that free martini."

Once they got into the boat, Janet asked the Haitian how long the ride was to the island. He curtly replied, "about an hour."

"In that case," Keith said, "we're going down into the birth. Wake us up ten minutes before we dock. The Haitian acknowledged Keith's order with a grunt.

It had been about eight or nine hours since Keith and his wife had eaten, so he searched through the cabinets in the tiny kitchenette and found a couple cans of sardines, a jar of grape jam, and a box of crackers. Not very appetizing he thought, but it would have to do.

The high-shrilling racket of the motorboat kept them from getting any sleep, so they returned to the stern of the boat and sat on the vinyl seats as the boat cut through the choppy water. The night was perfectly clear, and the stars shone especially bright. Keith was amazed by the clarity of the sky as they left the blurred city lights far behind in the spray of the motorboat's wake. They had gone, perhaps, twenty-five miles, when several tiny lights in the darkness began to sparkle in the distance over the bow. They were approaching Belski's home island, Beth-Gellert Isle.

The lights eventually disappeared from interference of the trees as they got closer to the island. The moon was nearly three-quarters full, and it cast a pale, soft light over the eerie landscape. A single electric lamp hanging from a tall pole illuminated the dock, which made it look like a twisted tongue lapping up the water around it. There were two outboard Sea Ray boats tied to the dock, and Keith wondered if they belonged to other visitors Belski may have invited to join them. When the Haitian cut the engine, the ambient sound of palm leaves flapping in the gentle breeze slowly began to replace the buzzing in Keith's ears. He watched the Haitian make several futile attempts at reaching for the rope dangling from one of the dock poles. Keith thought he appeared pathetic, and contrary to what would be one of his normal responses to help, he decided not to offer his assistance out of spite for the man's rudeness.

Eventually, their tenacious host was able to grasp the rope with his small, pudgy hands and pull the boat in. Once the boat was secure, he motioned for Keith and Janis to climb out of it onto the dock.

"Watch yourselves," he fussed, as he secured the rope.

Once the three of them were on the dock, Keith picked up his satchel. The Haitian insisted on carrying the rest, not that there was much, and they followed him onto the beach. Instead of soft sand, the ground was hard and damp. As they gained the foot of a small dune, it appeared to Keith that the breeze, which appeared so cheerfully on the beach, suddenly stopped. The palm leaves lay still, almost lifeless.

Walking on a narrow path, flanked by wet leaves and vines, the Haitian forced a brisk pace. Janis got swatted in the face by a whipping branch that unintentionally flicked off their guide's back. She wondered why he was in such a hurry to get them to their destination. Keith hesitated to ask him how far away they were from Belski's residence, presupposing he would get a snotty answer, if any at all. Nevertheless, just as he cleared his throat to poise the question, a small clearing appeared at the end of the claustrophobic trail.

Sixty paces ahead of them, behind a gigantic in-ground pool, with a 10-foot-high fence around its perimeter, stood what appeared to be a three-story Victorian-style house, complete with gables and a porch stretching along the front of the building. "He's all class, this Belski," Keith thought to himself. The house appeared foreboding in the sprawling shadows that fell across its multi-faceted structure. Notably, only two windows on the ground floor were lit up.

"What a crazy day it's been," Keith whispered to his wife. The Haitian practically forced his charges to jog as they passed the pool. He abruptly halted just before the fence, fumbled for a key from a chain around his neck, and awkwardly unlocked the gate in almost total darkness. Janis looked up to her husband with a puzzled expression. He reassured her with a patient smile, and then rolled his eyes in contempt for their ill-mannered guide.

Once through the gate, they were led through a brick walkway leading to the porch, where it abruptly ended in a long flight of shallow steps to the enormous, well-lit front door. While their guide fumbled for another key from the chain, Keith looked back toward the gate, and noticed that the pool they passed was black. It was obviously empty since no reflection of the moon and stars flickered from a watery surface.

With a sudden clang, the bolt of the lock in the door receded, and the man led them into a huge hall. Once inside, he pressed a button. The room was immediately flooded with spectacular light from a beautiful chandelier, dangling high above their heads from a timber which ran perpendicular to the front door. Squinting, Janis noticed the light splintered into thousands of brilliant reflections that shared some light with another room to the right. A draft drifted through the chandelier, provoking the delicate shards of crystal to send pleasing chords of soft clinking sounds through the cavernous room. Her dilated pupils slowly constricted as her eyes became accustomed to the light, and she began to relax from the pleasant surroundings.

"We finally made it, honey," Janis said, elbowing her husband.

"I wonder . . . " he groaned.

Though it was now early in the morning, their guide instructed them to wait where they stood with more asperity than was requisite. He dropped the luggage and headed to the left of the staircase. Locating a narrow door, he went through it and closed it behind him without a word.

"Is he coming back?" Janis asked her husband.

"I don't think so," he replied, shaking his head. "Maybe he went to get the good doctor."

While they waited, they strolled through the huge hall and admired the large, beautiful paintings of English fox hunts, luminous country dances, and still life's that hung on the walls. Large flags hanging from the ceiling and adorned with what looked like family crests gently moved in the draft high above. To the right of the staircase, an open door revealed an absence of steps, and instead, a ramp led to a lower floor, similar to handicap ramps in public buildings and hospitals for persons in wheelchairs. Through this door, and in the shadows beyond,

Keith noticed another enormous chamber, with a partial suit of armor exposed by the streams of artificial light trickling in from the hall.

"It must have taken years to design and construct this incredibly gorgeous home," Janis remarked.

"Yeah, the logistics must have been an ordeal getting everything from the mainland over here," he added.

"I wonder where Dr. Belski is," Janis said.

"I'm sure he'll be along soon, Keith guessed.

"Indeed," a baritone voice with a slight Russian accent bellowed from the top of the stairs.

Janis and Keith jerked their heads upward toward the top landing of the staircase and finally saw their host, a middle-aged man holding a cigar in one hand and a glass of scotch in the other. He was elegantly dressed in a white shirt, paisley silk jacket, white pants, and matching shoes. His salt and pepper hair was combed back, grayer on the sides than throughout the slicked back tresses at the top of his head. He had a devilish-looking goatee and mustache, and his brows slanted downward toward the bridge of his nose making him appear like he had a permanent scowl. An eye patch covered his right eye, and his teeth were heavily stained yellow, ostensibly from a lifetime of smoking. He proceeded to step down the stairs with a pronounced limp until he reached the lower landing.

"I am delighted you were able to make it," he said with a toothy grin.

Suddenly the little man came through the door he had disappeared through earlier. He pushed an electric-powered wheelchair over to Dr. Belski, assisted him into it and then stood beside him ready for instructions.

"It's so hard to get good help these days," Dr. Belski said, but Mr. Shirley is a real gem. I trust he took good care of you on your trip here?"

"Yes, of course," Keith lied through his teeth.

"Mr. Shirley goes by the name of Wheezer; please call him Wheezer; no need to be formal here. You may have noticed he doesn't talk much. He's a simple man but he's very capable. Isn't that right, Wheezer," Dr. Belski asked him. "See? He doesn't even answer me, and I'm his employer." He chuckled loudly in a cloud of bluish cigar smoke.

"Well, it's very nice to finally meet you, Dr. Belski," Janis said, walking up to shake his hand.

"And it is a privilege to have you both here. I am thrilled you made time in your hectic schedules to stop by for a few days. Wheezer will bring you upstairs to your room shortly, but I imagine you both must be famished."

"We are a little hungry, actually" Keith said, shaking the doctor's hand with a broad smile.

"Well then, let's get you two into the dining room and Wheezer will bring you some cold cuts and a nice wine. I apologize I don't have anything healthier to offer you, but I'm afraid we already had our dinner."

"Sandwiches and wine sounds perfect to us," Janis said. "Please don't go to any trouble."

"No trouble at all," Dr. Belski replied. "Follow me."

Dr. Belski led them into the next room with a large dining room table. The motion-sensing lights came on automatically. Wheezer went through a swinging door into the kitchen to put together the simple meal. Dr. Belski asked Janis and Keith to find a seat at the table.

"I'm not going to keep you kids up much longer, and I am sure you are exhausted, but before I retire to bed myself, I just want to kindly ask you to remain in your room until breakfast, which will be served at 8:00. You will love the room. It has lots of space, a full bath, and a beautiful view of the ocean, which you'll appreciate better in the morning. I will meet you for breakfast in the morning, and then we can get down to business. Does this sound OK?"

"Absolutely, Sir," Keith said.

"Oh, and one more thing, please don't call me 'Sir' or 'Dr. Belski.' We don't need all of this formality between us. I'd like you to treat me as your friend, so please call me Val, which rolls off the tongue a little easier than Valter."

"OK, Val . . . " Keith acknowledged with a grin.

After eating their sandwiches while Val talked about his house and his islands, Keith and Janis went up the stairs to their bedroom, and it was indeed, everything Val said it was. Aside from the large, cozy bed, there was also a roll top desk near the bay window with a computer on it.

"For the most part, I guess we'll be living out of this room for the next few days," Keith surmised.

"It'll be fine," Janis said, taking off her clothes. "Let's get to bed. It's already 2:00, so this should give us at least five hours of sleep."

After an uneventful rest, the alarm went off at seven, and they both took a shower and got dressed for breakfast.

"Do you know how he became an invalid?" Keith asked his wife.

"He had an accident when he lived in Freeport, Bahamas about four years ago. He purchased one of those pocket houses . . . "

"Pocket house?"

"Yes, it's how most of the islanders with some money build their homes, literally, out of their pockets. They cannot get a loan from the banks, so they save up their money and build as much of their house as they can, such as the main structure of it, and then they work and save some more and when they have enough, they put up a roof and so on until they finally have a completed home. Some of these people eventually lose their jobs or die, and so the island is pockmarked with these incomplete pocket houses. Val selected one of them and completed it himself for next to nothing.

"The purpose of his tenure there was to develop a drug that could be used to treat people with extreme anger issues that can potentially lead to violent, criminal activity: homicide and rape, for instance. He received a generous grant from the US government to work on this initiative. I think if was called, 'the Redemption Project.' It was the government's fast track attempt at artificial rehabilitation using drugs instead of counseling and education in an effort to reduce crime in the United States and as a possible method of returning prisoners back into society as productive, law-abiding citizens.

"Apparently, he was having a degree of success with his experiments. One instance involved an aggressive, adult chimpanzee that had been an exotic pet to someone before turning on its owner and tearing off his face to eat it.

"Nice."

"For a time, there was a definite improvement in the chimp, such that Val eventually permitted it free reign of his house and the fenced-in yard. At the same time, there were rumors that he was experimenting on some of the impoverished islanders at the same time, which is how he lost his eye. He was attacked by a gang of suspicious islanders, and they almost beat him to death.

"After a while, and with such promise, the chimp unfortunately resorted back to its former nature and attacked the doctor. He sustained serious injuries to his right leg and lower back, which explains the limp and the wheelchair."

"Incredible."

"But it gets worse. The chimp escaped the compound by breaking through the ceiling of the outdoor fence and ended up mangling a young woman. She survived, but by this time, both the US and island governments were through with him. The island government eventually seized his house and banned him from setting foot on the Bahamas ever again. He spent a short while in New Zealand and then he decided to settle here in the Keys for good."

"You sure know your research, Jan," Keith said, pulling on his cargo shorts. "I suppose it wouldn't be a reach to think that he's still working on this formula here now?"

"I don't see why not. He'll be rich and famous if he's able to succeed. He was close to it with what he accomplished with the chimp before it went berserk."

"Obviously, a bad side-effect of the drug," Keith said.

When Keith and Janis walked into the brightly lit dining room, Val was already sitting at the head of the table, pulling a cigar out of the inside pocket of his crimson smoking jacket.

"Good morning!" he said cheerfully. "As you can see it is a beautiful day. Did you two get enough sleep?"

"Yes," Keith said, pulling out a chair for his wife. "The bed is really comfortable."

Val lit his cigar, and inhaling deeply, he looked at his visitors with an awkward pause.

"You know," he said, "you two are much younger than I thought you'd be. You are a very handsome couple, a very handsome couple, indeed."

"Thanks," Keith said, taking a seat for himself.

Hundreds of miles away, in a small parsonage attached to a white Presbyterian church with green shutters, a green door, and a modest steeple, lived a minister and his wife.

A weather-beaten placard hanging from a chain on a post to the walkway of the parsonage read, "Dr., Rev. Ralph Johnson, Psychiatrist,

1st Presbyterian Church, Hopewell, Virginia". In smaller print beneath it, it read, "Sunday Worship Service 9:30, Bible Study Tuesday Eve. 7:30."

The walkway was in disrepair. Roots from flanking trees had broken through the cracks in the asphalt surface. It led to the front door of the parsonage, a large, heavy door, almost too big for the house with its once beautifully stained wood grain, now painted over with green paint. Over the door there was a campy, hand-painted sign that read, "Bless This House."

Ralph was the minister of the small church for 35 years, as well as being the only Christian psychiatrist in the tri-city area of Colonial Heights, Petersburgh, and Hopewell, in proximity to Virginia's state capital of Richmond.

Since coming to the states from Africa in '67, he lived in the sleepy little town of Hopewell with his wife, Zelma, their two cats, "Tensing" and "Rascal," and a Great Dane, "Moocher." Ralph and his wife were both in their early sixties, and he was planning to retire in five years to their quaint summer home in Twin Mountains, New Hampshire.

Zelma had a bit of a weight problem. With her gigantic posterior, enormous neck and bulging eyes, she was an unattractive woman. Her mean-tempered disposition was equally as ugly, which seemed ironic for a preacher's wife.

Ralph was everything his wife was not: gregarious, kind, considerate, and long-suffering. For some odd reason, his wife's venomous tongue-lashings, constant nagging, and repeated reminders of his shortcomings were arrows that struck hard, but never sank in deep enough to poison his attitude, even with the passage of many years of her abuse.

She was not always this way. Early in their marriage, she was nice enough and supportive. However, after years of her husband's strict devotion to his congregation over her own needs, she slowly retreated from the marriage into a lonely world of resentment and bitterness. Hence, Ralph reconciled his marriage as a trial that he would be rewarded for in eternity, a blessing for his lifelong devotion and faithfulness to his wife, in spite of her ill will. At least, this is what he hoped.

Earlier that morning, a thunderstorm woke him up from a deep sleep. As he tossed and turned in his bed, Ralph was restless. In surrender, he finally opened his eyes, and lazily focused on the mountain that was his wife four feet away in her own bed, snoring away in her own kind of storm. Past the highest peak of blankets that covered her, he squinted through sleepy eyes at the bedroom's only window. As the outside came into focus, he could make out the large pine tree on their front lawn, glistening in the light of the outdoor street light. He rolled over onto his back and watched the shadows dance across his ceiling in spidery fragments. The alarm clock ticked regimentally, and though he did not care to look, he pondered the time: "feels like 2:30," he thought to himself, as he folded his hands atop his chest, wiggling his fingers in frustration. He opened his mouth to wield a long, noisy yawn, and then swallowed hard, his throat notably dry. He felt so alone in their small bedroom, the same one he and his wife shared for twenty-nine years. With a loud squeak of the worn-out springs of her bed, his wife rolled over onto her side. She mumbled something about money and returned to her snoring. He hated it when his wife snored. After a moment or two, he extended his arm, and started to run his fingers along the night table that rested between their beds in search of his wax earplugs. He felt his glasses, and along the way he fingered the loose change in the ashtray that had never been used for smoking but was instead used to hold his loose pocket change. He explored a glass of water with his wife's false teeth floating in it, a packet of chewing gum, and his Bible. At last, right behind the clock, he located the earplugs. He rolled them in his palms and then forced them into his ears. In the silence, he could hear his heart beat. It was beating faster than he believed it had cause to, and he knew why. He still hadn't come up with a topic for his sermon and wondered what he would say to his small congregation during his Sunday morning Worship Service.

 He finally fell back to sleep and woke up just before the sun began to rise. He decided to get out of bed rather than force another hour of sleep. This was the only way he could guarantee a full hour or two of peace and quiet before his wife woke up and planned how to ruin his day. He grabbed his Bible and snatched his robe draped over a chair on his way out of the bedroom. He poured coffee—still on the stove from the previous morning—into a soup mug and reheated it in the microwave, a habit that his wife detested. This "quiet time," as he called it, was his favorite time of the day. He opened his soft leather-bound Bible to the book of Mark. From the 16th chapter, and starting with the 14th verse, he began to read aloud: "Afterward, He appeared to the eleven themselves as they were reclining at the table; and He reproached them for their unbelief and hardness of heart, because they had not believed those who had seen Him after He had risen. And He said to them, 'Go into all the world and preach the gospel to all creation. He who has believed and has been baptized shall be saved; but he who has disbelieved shall be condemned.'"

Ralph took a sip of the tepid brew. The words that he read spoke to him like claps of thunder still sounding its knell around his house. He had been turning over and over in his mind what he should do about this nagging, sinking feeling in his heart as he considered his upcoming vacation. He felt an urgent need to reach out to those not fortunate enough to hear about his faith. He also thought about his obligations to his little church. They could not go without their shepherd for long. Who could he find to substitute for him for two weeks?

He had started out as a missionary in Africa, and he believed he had served his time; paid his dues, so to speak. This was followed by thirty-five years in the ministry, twenty-nine of them married to his wife, who most in his congregation referred to as 'a cold fish' behind her back. In just a few more short years, he would be physically unable to minister to his church, especially with his diabetes getting worse. He felt compelled to speak to his congregation on Sunday morning following the service about an extended leave of absence. He was already approved for two weeks, and he had never taken more than two weeks off each year in 35 years of ministry, but lately, he was always tired, and he feared he was burning out. He could use an additional week or two for more reading, study, and self-reflection, he thought. It could be a time to recharge his batteries. It would also give him and his wife more time to get away and spend some real quality time together, hoping it would improve her attitude.

Later that morning, after his wife scolded him for letting the coffee spill over in the microwave, and after she hammered him for making a mess of the nightstand, he waited until she settled down before informing her that a Communicant member was coming over for some counseling. To this she retorted, "Oh sure, another Saturday where you work and I wait around for you to spend a little time with me, that is, if there's any time left for me! I tell you what Ralph; you do what you gotta do, and I'll do what I gotta do. I'm not gonna just sit around waiting on you all day."

Ralph knew how to pick his battles, so in his usual, sheepish tone of voice, he told her it would be a short day in the office, and perhaps they could go to Dunkin' Donuts for a coffee and a danish in the afternoon. Vigorously wiping out the inside of the microwave with Windex and a paper towel, she ignored him.

His small office was down a short, narrow hallway beginning at the kitchen, and ending between the study and the front door entranceway where a large mirror hung on the wall to the right of the study door. He noticed his unhappy expression as he passed by it and turned to examine his face. Behind the thick lenses of his horn-rimmed glasses, his eyes were moist, and they looked glassy beneath the heavy eyelids that made him appear sad, he thought. Unshaven with sagging jowls, and almost completely bald, his face seemed shapeless to him.

As he stood there feeling sorry for himself, a scream from the bathroom came out as loud and clear as a pistol shot. "Ralph! There is pee all over the seat!" With the bathroom window wide open, he was certain their young neighbors, the Wallace's were laughing and hanging on every word from her ranting and raving mouth. "How many times have I told you to sit down on the toilet when you pee!"

"I'm no woman," he said under his breath to himself in the mirror. Then a terrible thought came into his head, but he forced himself to think of something else. "No honorable man, especially a man of God should think these thoughts." As dark as his thought was, it alarmingly had the effect of cheering him up a little but after his smile faded, he felt remorseful for letting it linger in his mind as long as it did.

"Sorry about that babe!" he shouted, "I won't let it happen again!"

Among the two or three flushings of the toilet, she ignored him.

"Frankenstein," Val observed, exhaling a pillar of smoke from his cigar, "is a reincarnation of the Golem, really. A young woman's dreamed-up masterpiece spawned from a rainy night of alcohol-induced conversations centered around old French ghost stories," he continued.

"Together with her poet husband at the Villa Diodati, they were visited by the confused and unscrupulous Dr. Polidori, and his onetime patient, the "bad and dangerous to know," Lord Byron, the romantic poet. The quartet challenged one another to write a ghost story, which was to be read aloud, if I remember the story correctly," he added.

"Yes, I read that book when I was around twelve," Keith said, sharing a hidden look of confusion with his wife.

"In the Summer of 1816," Val said, continuing his story. "the warm and humid weather suddenly turned raw. The relentless rains drove them indoors for much of their time together, where discussions of such things created a certain mood; precarious and perhaps a little gloomy.

"In an atmosphere of sexual experimentation with feelings of guilt and excitement that soldered their bonds in an alliance of free love and intellectual discourse, there was a certain pathless and graceless slope leading them to a certain evening when, in the shadows, they each birthed a ghost story in the spirit of competition.

"Frankenstein has captivated readers of every generation in its eerie narrative—why?"

Feeling a bit put on the spot, and not knowing where this weird conversation was going, Keith said, "It's the creation of a literary genius. There is no other story like it."

"Wrong!" Val shouted, pulling the cigar out of his whiskered mouth. "In Shelley's day, there was a certain scientist, a Dr. Erasmus Darwin, grandfather of the evolutionist, who planted the scientific seed of reason that would soon grow to strangle the life from popular dogmas of the times. The suggestion he offered for consideration was that it might be possible to duplicate certain characteristics of human life in a controlled, scientific environment without God's help, without His blessing, and without His permission. Such thoughts would have been received as blatant heresy, but what blasphemous ideas must have thundered in that man's brain! If for no other accomplishment, his name will forever be remembered when he set the wheels of spontaneous generation in motion when he made a mere string of spaghetti move on its own!

"Think of it, Janis," Val exclaimed, "spontaneous generation, which was a widely published discovery at the time, made Frankenstein a popular horror yarn instead of the profane, underground pamphlet that it would have been otherwise received."

Janis was not sure what to make of Val's sudden commentary at the breakfast table. She was as confused as Keith. Val sensed this and smiled mischievously.

"Can I show you two something?" he teased.

"Of course, Val," Keith said, finishing his coffee.

Using the small joystick on the arm of his wheelchair, Val led Keith and Janis down a hall off the dining room into a large laboratory. Everything in the room was state-of-the-art. Keith and Janis could hear the sounds of animals in the distance. Perceiving this, Val explained that he had as assortment of apes, big cats, pigs, and rodents in an adjoining room. Obviously, he was using these for his continuing experiments to discover a formula that could be used to alter, or more specifically, reduce aggression in humans. Though she had never met him before the previous night, Janis assumed she might share a particular bond with Val, professionally speaking. She read most of his books and articles and viewed a few of his documentaries based on his work with animals beginning in the late eighties and throughout the nineties. Though he played a large part in the development of cloning, he was never given any credit, but this did not seem to bother him, as he invested all of his resources into a more important work.

In recent years, medical journals and white papers have not done much more than to highlight his failures in other endeavors, such as in his attempts to develop a hormone which would provide humankind with an enhanced mental stamina with respect to memory and calculation, as well as increases to physical strength.

His work in Scotland during the discovery of cloning left him disillusioned for a while, but he has since put it behind him. Now he lives on his own island, one of three that he owns outright, where he is free to do as he pleases with no interference from the outside world, which is why she was surprised by his invitation three weeks ago; he still hadn't explained the purpose of their visit.

As he gave them a tour of his facilities, she could not help but notice how much older he appeared than his age. He dressed sharply, smoked Cuban cigars, and drank the best single malt Scotch whiskies available, but she could not help but feel that his loud outbursts over breakfast were attempts at disguising his weaknesses by appearing lucid and strong. Why else would he have reached out to her? For a very brief moment, she wondered if his experiments were centered on improving his own physical condition and mental health more than the original intent of serving humankind overall.

He interrupted her thoughts with a question: "Do you know anything of the supernatural, my dear? Persons of perception are hard to find."

"I'm afraid it isn't one of my fortes, Val, but Keith has some experience with parapsychology and the occult."

Turning his attention to Keith, Val asked him to what degree he was familiar with the supernatural. Keith responded that he was more 'book smart' than he was experienced with actual situations involving the supernatural.

"Well, that's fine, Keith," Val said, looking up to him from his wheelchair. "You will be even more interested in my work then."

"Why is that, Val?" Keith asked.

"Where science fails to explain the unexplainable from an emotional or spiritual perspective, I have found that spiritualism, whether of an orthodox Christian/Judeo belief system, or of the occult, helps to provide answers where science and technology fail to deliver."

While engaged in conversation, Wheezer suddenly entered the room with a tray of fruit, cheese and sparkling water, setting it down on a table near Val.

"You take this pomegranate," Val said, as he thrust a knife into the fruit, "it has an utterly useless and inedible shell, but inside, the meat is vibrantly red and firm—pleasing to the eye—and the juice from the meat is sweet and succulent. There is no fruit lovelier to the taste, or more sensual to the eyes. Surely, this was the fruit the serpent used to tempt Eve, and not the ordinary apple. Every time I taste these tiny beads of sweet benediction, it is as though I rediscover its flavor all over again. Similar to perceiving your likeness in the mirror and then forgetting what you look like as soon as you walk away. How reassuring it is to rediscover your face time and time again, much as it is for me when enjoying this wonderful pomegranate.

"In this example that I am sharing with you, it equates to the feeling of discovery within the field of science, do you follow? Discovery enlightens the eyes, the smell, the taste, and the soul, but the conquest mesmerizes the senses in a swirl of temporary sensuality. The challenge, the conquest, the sheer delight in reveling in the creation—or discovery—of your work; is there anything that delights the senses more than this? But standing still in an accomplishment is sheer agony to me, so I am driven to keep moving forward; pushing the envelope; challenging myself to unleash the success of another new discovery. For example, you hear a lovely song on the piano, and you cannot rest until you learn it and practice it until you get it perfect, but once you do, you want to slit your wrists from the utter boredom of it. Such is my desire to learn the secrets of the universe, ever pressing me forward and keeping from ever standing still in one place or in a particular success.

"As you both know, especially yourself, Janis, I was born to controversy. How else could I have found myself in self-imposed exile in order to work through the kinds of undertakings that others would never for a moment consider touching? It is like the forbidden fruit in the garden; they leave it alone, but if you dare take a bite out of that fruit, you become like God and gain the knowledge of good and evil!

"When I was younger, I could no more embrace conventional practices of science than profess blind adherence to any religion, which I saw as hypocritical and the mechanism for a life filled with guilt, remorse and regret. I suppose I forced myself into a position of religious and political agnosticism. As a scientist, I detested hypocrisy and inanity, and I recognized the impediments in scientific advances by seeing the fissures between education and religion.

"However, I've come to recognize that I am as much a spiritual being as I am a physical one and I see this as an area not seriously considered in science. What is the body, after all, but flesh, blood, bone, and the soul . . . "?

Looking at the tiger lilies reaching up to his office window, Ralph shook his head and laughed about the fleeting thought of murdering his wife. "What's wrong with me," he thought.

At about 11:00, his appointment with a 17-year-old girl and her father arrived. Her name was Dedre Taylor, and for all Ralph knew of her from his parish, she was an ordinary, pleasant enough young woman with a kind, round face, and almond-shaped eyes. Her father, Elmer, was once a deacon of the church, but he resigned shortly after the death of his wife from an automobile accident the previous year. He was having trouble with his daughter, but nothing involving drugs or alcohol. Ralph surmised the grief they were suffering with the death of his wife—her mother—was demanding on his dual role now as both parents, and as a consequence, she began to drift from him, identifying more with her teenage peers and all of their problems with authority and the challenges facing them as adults.

Ralph warmly greeted them at the door, and showing them to his office, he sat them down across from his desk and got the interview underway. The young girl explained how she frequently suffered from bouts of depression, and more recently, a deep sense of impending death. These types of feelings were common enough with teens based on his general experience with them, but they got Ralph's attention when her father mentioned something that was indeed, out of the ordinary. The reason he sought a consultation was because of recent visitations she was getting at night—from malevolent apparitions.

He explained that though she was involved with the Communicant's class for membership to the church, she suddenly had no desire for prayer or reading the Bible, and though at times she wished to be a "good Christian like her mother was," she also had a revulsion against such a sentiment.

One evening earlier in the week, she awoke and found herself desperately fighting to free herself from the embrace of cold, ghostly hands around her throat. She explained that she and her new friends had begun to play around with Tarot cards. Her curious interest in them incited a desire to steal events of her future, such that would save her and her father from a fate similar to her mother's untimely demise. Apparently, she had a reasonable motive, but I advised her that it was a wrong one.

Ralph was familiar with the black arts himself from the superstitious inclination of the Bauchi, Nigerian people he grew up with. When he was fourteen, a hurricane had wiped out much of the area, and the United States government and other groups of volunteers from Canada and Europe sent relief in terms of people and financial aid to help get the town and other neighboring areas back on their feet again. One of the Americans, a member of the Peace Corps, assisted with this rebuilding effort and in the process, he took an interest in the young people, himself being about twenty years of age.

At the time, the Bauchi suicide rate among teenage girls was nearly 30%. The catastrophe of the hurricane seemed to bring out the worst in many of the men, so kidnappings, rape and murder escalated into a profoundly serious problem. Ralph would never forget the impact the Americans impressed upon his extended family, so much that, at the age of sixteen, he said his goodbyes and joined the Peace Corps himself, leaving with them when they returned to the States.

After graduating from a New England college, he attended seminary, and when he turned twenty-seven, he was ordained as a

Presbyterian minister. He later went back to school and got his PhD in Psychiatry. For the better part of 35 years, he was a church planter, first in New England, and now in the South. He loved his work in the church and family counseling. His work was the only real enjoyment he had left now that he was approaching retirement.

Unfortunately, he could not help everyone, including himself, ironically, with a broken marriage, such as it was. All of his religious and psychiatric training had not benefitted his own relationship with a troublesome wife, but his faith taught him that there was still hope, and as long as there was hope, he continued to believe that there were some people that he could help.

Later, after a private interview with the girl, he excused her so that he could meet privately with her father, after which time he would meet with them both again. Ralph informed Elmer that apart from the oppressive and otherworldly distress his daughter was experiencing in recent days, she appeared as normal as any other teenage girl on the cusp of adulthood.

The interview revealed that she was not experiencing any other unsettling traumas, such as a broken relationship, a flirtation with drugs or alcohol, or chaos within the family outside of missing her mother. She seemed the sole member of the family subjected to this inner turmoil.

The occult was becoming a bit of a fad among young people. Kids just want to find meaning to their lives and they look for answers the easy way, but not the reliable way. Ralph asked her directly if she had any direct involvement with the occult aside from Tarot card readings, and she denied any such activities. She could have been lying, which if she were, would interfere with his help but all Ralph could do was give her the benefit of the doubt.

During the interview, Elmer mentioned that there was an incident that took place in his own past that he was never happy about. It seems his daughter started to menstruate very early, at age nine, and suffered miserably each cycle of the month. After a couple of years of this, Elmer's wife, in a weak moment in her own faith and devotion to God, brought her to a new age practitioner after several doctors could do nothing to help their daughter. This practitioner had a rented office in Richmond, and on three or four occasions, this woman administered a potion that was intended to protect Dedre from the evil spirts who were attacking her with the agony she experienced each month. This "white witch" also gave her a fetish—a charm—to wear around her hips so that the amulet rested against her private area during the days of menstruation. This she did, as instructed, for eight years, until she lost it swimming in a lake two months ago on a camping trip. Ralph explained that the healing method of this spiritualist preyed on the subconscious, and not on the physical malady itself. It was a cheap trick. The result of placing so much faith in such a false "cure," had permitted its influence to passively capture her mind, where not only did emotional disturbances manifest itself, but her ability to make any religious decision became compromised by her belief in the charm. It came down to either she believed in God, or she believed in the fetish. Since she placed so much faith in the charm, it was her belief—or wishful thinking—that addressed the pain. It is all psychological, you see. She could have done the same thing with her faith in Christ, except she could no longer depend on prayer as a source of true healing, and instead, she depended on her own powers of the mind to trick her into thinking the charm was working to protect her. Meanwhile, during the years that she was depending on this charm to relieve her pain, the root of her physical issue was ignored and never addressed. Had her mother taken more time to source competent physicians when she was nine or ten, the real source of the problem would have been discovered and then proper medical help could have been provided via corrective surgery or management of it with proper drug therapy. Now that the amulet is gone forever in the depths of a lake, so is the reason for her to continue believing in it, and so the pain, which was always present—at least, in some degree—can now manifest itself as it did before this meddling in the occult, which was initiated by Elmer's wife.

With Elmer's permission, Ralph continued the next phase of his interview of the girl. He explained to Dedre that she should renounce her belief placed in charms and renew her relationship with God. Ralph also asked her father to seek out a qualified gynecologist to medically alleviate his daughter's painful condition, which could have been pointing to something more serious all along.

After thanking Ralph for his help, he ushered them to the front door where he bid them goodbye. Ralph's wife, who had been sulking in the kitchen the entire time, stuck her head into the hallway, and bid them goodbye in that insincere falsetto tone of voice that Ralph loathed so much.

At the door, the young woman asked her father to go on ahead so that she could speak to Ralph for another minute in private. Elmer obliged and Ralph stood in the entranceway anticipating whatever it was that she wanted to say.

"Rev. Johnson," Dedre whispered, knowing that his wife was listening from the kitchen.

"Yes, Dear?" he said, letting the screen door close. "What is it?"

"I know you will not appreciate what I have to say because it involves the Tarot cards, but I feel compelled to tell you something."

"Go ahead," Ralph said softly.

"The cards . . . I did not initially want to come here . . . my father forced me to come, but now I am glad I did. I'm sorry, and I feel a little weird about this, but the cards told me so many things. Sometimes they were right and other times they were wrong. They were often vague. Yet, even when the interpretation was vague, there seemed to be a kernel of truth in it, and though I reject the cards now, I am bothered by something they revealed to me."

"Dedre, you do not need to tell me about it because, to your point, these readings are so vague, that any interpretation could point to just about any outcome."

"And if they didn't reveal to me what they did, then I could deny them a little easier, but in this particular reading, the future from this particular reading of the cards was yours."

"Me?" Ralph asked her, jerking his head back in surprise.

"Yes, Reverend," she said, running her fingers through her hair. "My friends and I . . . we were just fooling around with the cards one night. I confided with them that my father was bringing me to see you for counseling that I did not want. As I was laying the cards out on my bed, they indicated that you were either already in terrible danger, or that you were going to be."

Ralph laughed nervously. He secretly wanted the girl to specify whether it was he who was in danger, or more to the point—his wife. Indeed, he was not interested in what the cards may have determined in their dubious configuration, but he could not help but be intrigued. Regardless, with this revelation off her chest, he believed she might more willingly put them away for good and embrace her former faith.

"I am both happy and relieved that you have decided to forsake these cards and charms, Dedre, because if you consider looking at the occult from a scientific point of view, where there is no basis of scientific law in the pursuits of these fetishes, the ambiguity of these predictions leave all sorts of possibilities open. The point you made about the vagueness of such things . . . this should be enough to persuade you of their meaninglessness. Worse than this, the potential risk is that you would try to change your future based on such vague readings, and that could cause all sorts of ramifications in your life. The person who seeks for answers from the Tarot, for instance, comes already with a certain degree of readiness to believe in whatever they reveal. Even if the cards appear true in the way they point to a revelation, your faith in them will lead you to seek more suggestive influences. This subjective fulfillment is an escape to a blind alley of mediumistic entanglement, and it almost always leads to bondage. Look at you now, you are free."

The girl smiled broadly.

"Thank-you, Reverend Johnson," she said. "I guess the whole thing sounds silly; I just feel better getting it off my chest."

"That's great, Dedre," Ralph reassured her. "Will I see you with your Dad in church tomorrow?"

"Absolutely."

Ralph watched her climb into her father's pickup truck, and with a wave and a beep of the horn, they were gone.

Val discussed his work with Janis and Keith with great enthusiasm until noon, when it was time for lunch. Val suggested they walk back to the dining room. A meal would already be waiting for them, laid out by Wheezer. Val was going to work through lunch and meet up with them for dinner. In the meantime, he suggested they relax and take a hike around the island and perhaps, spend some time on the beach as they would have it all to themselves.

After lunch, this was exactly what Keith and Janis decided to do. They hiked to the highest point of the island and saw the other two islands owned by Val. The one furthest away appeared to be out ten miles or so, with the one closest to them no more than a fifteen-minute boat trip.

They spent much of the afternoon hiking around the highest areas of the island, collecting insects, a handful of interestingly colored stones, and an old, broken machete that someone had forgotten to bring back with them for what seemed like a long time, considering the weathered condition of it.

On the way down a gradual slope leading to a beach, Keith tripped over something protruding from the ground, a root, or a rock, he thought. Getting back on his feet and brushing himself off, Janis identified the source of his fall by pulling a long-handled spade out of the dead palm leaves along the path. "What would this be doing up here," she wondered aloud.

"Probably left by the same person who forgot the machete," Keith proposed.

"I don't think so," Jane said. "Not that it matters, but the machete is old and rusted, whereas this shovel actually looks quite new, almost unused."

Inspecting the shovel closer, Keith had to agree.

"Strange how it was just left here, so far from the house," Janis remarked.

Keith looked around but did not see any holes or other reason for it being there. "Must have just fallen off someone's backpack on the way up or down this hill," Keith surmised. "May as well get started back. We can give these to Wheezer. Perhaps he knows something about them, at least the shovel, anyway."

As they left the scene to return back to the main house, they had not noticed the mound of earth just four feet away from them in the shade of coconut trees.

Keith and Janis went to the dining room an hour before dinner would be served.

"I could use a cold bottle of water, but Wheezer's nowhere in sight. How about a cold bottle of spring water?" Keith asked his wife.

"Sure," she answered.

"I'll be right back. I'm sure Wheezer would not mind if I went into the kitchen's refrigerator.

Keith pushed through the swinging door that separated the dining room and kitchen and called out for Wheezer. Getting no response, he walked over to the refrigerator to get a couple bottles of Perrier. When he opened the door, he was immediately taken aback from the amount of food in it. Curiously, he opened the freezer door, and it was just as loaded with food. Over against the wall there was a walk-in freezer with a window on it. He looked through it and flipping the light switch on, he was astounded by the sheer volume of meats and other food supplies inside. He looked over his shoulder for any sign of Wheezer and not getting one, he opened several cabinet doors along the walls of the kitchen and found dozens of plates, cups, and large serving bowls, which he thought was odd considering that only the professor and his servant lived in the house.

On his way back through the swinging door, he handed his wife one of the bottles. "Here you go," he said, taking a sip from his own. "I know it's probably nothing, but you should see the amount of food Val has crammed into his refrigerator and freezers."

"Why would that be strange?" she asked. "We're on a remote island."

"I know that darling, but the mainland is only 90 minutes away and there's enough food in there to last Val and Wheezer for three years. They even have two sides of beef hanging in the walk-in freezer."

"You must have forgotten about the animals we heard earlier today—remember the room off the lab?"

"Oh, that's right," Keith said, shaking his head. "Why didn't I think of that. Of course . . . the animals . . . I suppose they gotta eat too."

A half hour later, Keith heard the whirring of Val's electric wheelchair coming down the hall toward the dining room.

"He's coming," Keith told his wife.

Val entered the dining room and noticed the two empty bottles of Perrier on the table.

"So, how do you like the island?" he inquired.

"It's so beautiful here, Val," Janis said. "The views from the top of the island are breathtaking. We also saw your two other islands."

"Yes, the one closest to us is exclusively for my animals. Some of them have free reign, but most are kept in cages and specially constructed enclosures. Wheezer went over there this morning to feed them but should be back anytime now. Are you alright with cold pheasant under glass?"

"Sounds great," Keith said, relishing the thought.

"Would you be so kind as to bring me a bottle of water too?" Val slyly asked Keith.

Feeling a little guilty about having possibly taken advantage of his host by going into his kitchen without permission, Keith went through the swinging door and returned with a bottle of Perrier.

"You'll find a glass in the hutch," Val said, pointing to it against the dining room wall.

"You're finding your way around the property I see," Val said, taking the glass from Keith.

"Yes, Val," Keith replied softly.

"I suppose I should have made this clear early on," Val said, pouring the water into his glass. He paused and looked intently into Keith's eyes as though to read his mind. Not laboring the pause any longer, he said, "but I should ask you both to keep to the dining room, the den, and your bedroom during your visit, and I only make this request for your well-being. Wheezer doesn't like anyone in his kitchen—he doesn't even want me in there—and since you are not familiar with the layout of my home, it is best that you permit me to set this boundary."

"Please accept my apologies," Keith implored. "You're right, I should have asked permission before helping myself."

"No problem, lad, and no apology necessary. It's my fault that I didn't make this clear to you from the beginning. I only make this request because I have some expensive equipment throughout the house and since most of it is irreplaceable, I think it would be best if you were not to venture outside these rooms just for safety's sake."

"I totally get it, Val. No worries."

"Alright, enough of this," Val said, just as Wheezer entered the dining room with a large tray. "I skipped lunch, so let's dig in, I'm absolutely famished."

After dinner, Val invited Keith and Janis to join him in the large den for more conversation related to his work. Settling into an Italian leather couch, Val approached them in his wheelchair and offered Keith a cigar. Keith wasn't a smoker, but he didn't want to insult his host, so he took it and put it into his mouth.

"You'll need to bite of a tiny bit off the end first, son, or you won't be able to smoke it."

Feeling ridiculous, Keith complied, but he bit off a bit too much and pulled out pieces of tobacco from his mouth.

"Not a cigar smoker, I see," Val chuckled. "Though I'm used to them, you won't want to inhale these," he said, lighting the tip of it.

Regardless, Keith still coughed from the giant cloud he created from the large hole he made, to the amusement of Val. Janis could not help from joining in with the laughter, herself.

Val poured three glasses of brandy on the coffee table between them and asked them to join him in a toast.

"Here's to Keith, that he may live the night after finishing his cigar."

The three of them shared another laugh at his expense, but he was not embarrassed at all. In fact, he was relieved, since it took attention away from Val's mild reproach before dinner.

Janis took a sip of brandy and asked Val if she could ask him a question, to which he encouraged.

"Keith and I were exploring the island earlier this afternoon and we came across a discarded machete that looked like it had laid on the ground for years, and on the way down to the beach, we stumbled over a shovel, which looks practically brand new. We were wondering if there were other people on the island."

"I was going to go into this a little later, but yes and no," Val said, abruptly. The four of us, that is, you and Keith, myself and Wheezer are the only ones on this island, which I refer to as the main island. The island closest to us, Neo, is where I keep my animals, as I mentioned before, and on the island furthest away, Subbu, I sometimes permit people to vacation on it to help bring in a little more income. I don't have anyone lodging there now, but by the time spring arrives, I open it up to vacationers and tourists; even spring breakers from some of the more prestigious colleges in America and the UK. I do not advertise it, but those who rent my cottages are typically repeat clients that I have known for a while now. Perhaps you'd like a tour of Neo tomorrow?" Val offered.

"That would be wonderful," Janis said enthusiastically. "Wouldn't it, Keith?"

"Absolutely, but not if it's too much trouble," Keith added.

"No trouble at all since I need to see the animals from time to time anyway, but since there's nothing to see on Subbu, we'll leave that off the tour."

"Perhaps someday we too can rent one of your cottages on Subbu," Janis suggested, reaching for Keith's hand.

"Perhaps," Val said, finishing off his brandy.

Ralph knew his wife was eavesdropping the entire time in the kitchen, and the last place he wanted to be right now was anywhere around her, but she heard the door close and the truck drive away, so knowing he was finished for the day, she beckoned for him to join her for lunch. As he suspected, she wanted to know everything that transpired between them, but he told her that he was not at liberty to discuss any of it with her, which she interpreted as disrespect and a lack of trust. Ralph had been through this tired old argument many times before, so he did what he usually does and tried to think of something that would change the direction of the conversation and get his wife off the subject.

"You know what we need, honey?" he said.

"What?" she snapped back.

"You know this vacation we're taking?"

"Yeah."

"Let's so something completely different. Forget about spending our vacation in the New Hampshire woods with the mosquitoes and the rain. Let's take a proper vacation and go somewhere really pleasant and warm, like the Florida Keys. We can rent one of those tropical huts they have on stilts in the water with nothing but blue sea and sky around us in all directions. We can rent a boat and go sightseeing and swim in the warm water of the beaches."

"A Florida vacation?" his wife said, raising her voice, excitedly. "You'd take me to Florida? For two weeks? But what about your studies? What about New Hampshire?"

"Let's make this vacation all about us, honey. Let's just get out of here and go someplace warm and beautiful and leave all our troubles behind for a couple of weeks. We can use this time to get recharged and spend the whole time together."

"I'm in! Let's do it!"

Having extracted himself from another fight with his wife, Ralph ate his ham and cheese sandwich and took a beer with him back to his office. Feeling defeated, he knew what he was giving up—a couple of weeks catching up on his reading and an opportunity to finish the first draft of his second book, but after thinking about it for a while, he was actually looking forward to a couple of weeks on the beach doing nothing but relaxing. Even with his wife along, he knew she would be bored after two days of it and would want to spend time in the city shopping and eating at the myriad restaurants that catered to tourists. This would give him time to actually do some reading and writing, so perhaps, this was not a bad idea after all. He would shelve the request for an extended furlough, at least for now.

A couple of weeks later, with all of the preparations made, Ralph and his wife took a cab to the airport and flew to Sarasota. From there they took another cab to Long Boat Key where he charted a boat that cruised to the Lighthouse Resort. After a couple of days there, they took a short boat ride to Sand Crab Island where they rented a stilt house not far from the resort so that his wife could easily get a boat ride to the resort without him.

The next morning after breakfast, Val surprised the couple by asking Janis a question neither of them would have ever expected to hear.

"Janis, have you ever wondered what it would be like to fall asleep in the mane of a lion or lie down beside a tiger, tame as a kitten?"

Janis darted her eyes across the table to her husband, who returned her gaze with a puzzled expression of his own.

"I can't say that I ever have, Val, but that would be quite an experience."

"What if I could take you—right now—into my menagerie to walk in complete safety among all of my wild animals, each one of them loose without cages or other constraints?"

"I don't know what to say, Val."

"Just say that you'll follow me."

Val lead them to his laboratory and then to a door of a small room on the other side of it. He placed his right palm on a scanner and the door slid open. This was the nucleus of Val's estate, what he called the Control Room. It was equipped with computers, monitors, a surveillance camera system, and other electronics that Keith was unfamiliar with. Over a desk against the wall there was an open cabinet with several keys hanging inside. There was a handgun on the bottom shelf.

Separating the control room from the menagerie was a large, reinforced double-paned window. To their astonishment, Keith and Janis saw a variety of wild animals in another, much larger room, which is what Val referred to as his menagerie.

"Look how the lion and the tiger walk among the pigs and my cow," he exclaimed proudly.

"If I didn't see this with my own eyes, I'd never believe it," Keith said in awe.

"See the monkeys and the apes in their artificial trees above? Look at the gorilla! Have you seen anything like this?" Val asked excitedly.

"I'm speechless," Janis said, observing them.

"Keith, when I open the door to go inside, it will close by itself. The only way in or out is by way of a palm-reading scanner on both sides of it, and it is only programmed for mine and Wheezer's palms. I assure you, that I will be perfectly safe inside. I've done this dozens of times already. Trust me."

When Val placed his hand on the scanner, the door slid open, and he passed though it to the other side. The door swiftly closed shut behind him with a red LED light flashing over the hand scanner indicating that it was securely locked.

Keith and Janis observed the doctor negotiating his wheelchair among all of the animals inside the cavernous room. The tiger lazily meandered up to him and nuzzled him with its immense head, its 3-inch-long fangs protruding menacingly from its mouth.

"Can you hear me?" Val asked through the intercom.

"Yes, we can hear you, Val," Keith said, hardly believing his eyes.

Val grabbed hold of the tiger's mouth and gently forced it open. "You see these teeth?"

"Yes."

As you know, big cats in the wild do not normally hunt man as a common source of their diet, but they may attack if they cannot satisfy their needs otherwise. One telltale sign of a man-eating tiger is old or missing teeth. See his teeth? I guarantee you that this was once a man-eater yet look how playful he is with me. I'm perfectly safe."

"How is this possible, doctor?" Janis asked.

"It's my formula. I perfected it two months ago and for all the times I've been in here with my animals, not once has any of them shown the slightest aggression toward me."

"Your formula works!" Janis shouted.

"Yes, it works. Now I want you two to come in. Do not worry, they will not harm you. Keith, there is a loaded handgun in the cabinet to your left. Go ahead and take it with you if you have any concern over the safety of your wife and yourself, but believe me, you won't need it."

Keith was a realist and not typically one to take any chances, so he grabbed the handgun and waited with Janis at the door for Val to let them in with the scanning of his palm.

Once inside and with the door closed behind them, they clung close to each other. Keith inspected the gun and switched the safety off.

Val returned to the tiger, now sniffing a gorilla laying in a bed of straw. "Come in!" Val said. "Honestly, Keith, you don't need that weapon. You're as safe as a baby in her mother's arms. Come pat the tiger. Her name is Jemima. Come, come!"

Keith and Janis stepped toward the tiger as a single unit. When they stood three feet from it, Keith knelt on one knee and reached out his hand. The tiger left the gorilla alone and bowed its head for Keith to scratch. It purred loudly with pleasure and Keith told Janis that he could actually feel the vibrations of it all the way to his belly.

"I can't believe this is happening," Janis said.

"You see? I told you!" Val said triumphantly. "Now, if you think this is incredible, what until I show you my greatest achievement. Tomorrow morning, we go to Neo where you will be truly astounded."

Ralph and his wife sat outside their stilt house watching the sunset, one of the most spectacular ones they had ever seen.

"Let's rent a boat and go deep sea fishing in the morning," Ralph suggested.

"OK," his wife responded, much to his surprise. "I'll go along, but I don't really want to fish. I just want to go for the ride."

"No problem at all," Ralph said. "This will give us some real downtime. We'll pack a lunch and just spend the day cruising around the islands. Bring your camera too. There will be a lot of great opportunities to get some pictures of the islands and perhaps some wildlife around here."

"Good idea, I'll do that. Perhaps we'll even see some dolphins!"

The next morning, Ralph rented a 20-footer, and soon he and his wife were on their way. The fishing wasn't very good, much to Ralph's chagrin, but like he mentioned the night before, it was just a great time to unwind and relax in the sun with the gentle rising and falling of the ocean waves beneath them. After lunch, they both fell asleep from the mild rocking of the boat.

Two hours later, his wife woke him up shouting for him to start up the boat. As Ralph rubbed his eyes, he intuitively knew the reason. The sky was turning black with heavy clouds, and it looked like rain. The ocean was also giving signs of a possible storm as it rocked the boat back and forth like a toy. Ralph put away the fishing gear and fired up the boat to head back to the boat rental office, but not seeing land in any direction, he assumed they had drifted quite a ways out during their nap. He checked the GPS, and sure enough, they had drifted into deep sea. He instructed his wife to take a seat and cover herself with a poncho. It was going to be a rough ride back. Soon the clouds became darker, and lightning appeared in the distance. The waves were rising and sinking with greater force against the boat as he keep it on track for Sand Crab Island. Within 30 minutes, the lighting was overhead, and the rain came down in buckets. It seemed that for every ten feet he advanced through the choppy water, it pushed his boat back by twenty. He got on the radio and gave the coast guard their position. An hour later, he noticed that he was running out of gas, but he dared not alert his wife. The torrential rain didn't let up and he was convinced that they were going to be trapped in a tropical storm, which worried him because this meant they were just going to get pulled further out to sea. When the engine finally stopped, his wife demanded to know what the problem was. He told her that they had run out of gas.

"Well get on the radio again!" she shouted.

"I already did, but now I'm not getting a response," he told her. He tried it again, and all they could hear was static.

"So, what do we do now?" he wife cried.

"Listen, it's not as bad as you think," he said in an attempt to reassure her. This is a rock-solid boat, and the coast guard knows we're stranded out here. I also turned on the emergency locator beacon, so it is only a matter of time before they reach us, but in the meantime, let's pull the tarp over the boat and secure it as best we can to try and keep as much water out of it as possible. We're safe in the boat, but we'll just have to ride out the storm."

"Ride out the storm?" his wife shot back flippantly. "Ride out the storm? How long is that going to take?"

"I don't know, Zelma," he said, through foggy eyeglasses. It could just be a passing thunderstorm, but we need to make the boat as airtight as possible in case this tempest lingers.

They worked as a team, more than they have done in a long time. Once the boat was batted down, they laid on the floor beneath the tarp overhead holding hands and prayed for the storm to end or for the coast guard to reach them.

The storm lasted all night and when it finally ended, they removed the tarp from the boat to get a look around. Apparently, they drifted into a cluster of small islands, and lucky for them, they were being sucked in by the tide toward one with a sandy beach. Once they were close enough, Ralph climbed out of the boat and dragged it in as far as he could before the keel struck the sandy bottom of the shore, approximately twenty feet out.

He dropped the anchor and grabbed one end of the rope that was tied to the boat. "You'll have to climb out and swim with me to the beach, hon," he told her, expecting another argument over it. Surprisingly, she was only too happy to get her feet back on land, so she did exactly as he said and together, they swam to the beach. As soon as they got out of the water, Ralph tied the boat's rope to a palm tree.

"I need to go back and get our cooler. It is all the food and water we'll have until someone comes looking for us. In the meantime, go into the trees and try to get as comfortable as you can. I'll be right back."

"Check to see if the emergency beacon is still on and try the radio again," she said, as he checked the strength of the knot.

"I will."

When Ralph was able to get back into the boat, he gathered the cooler, the fishing gear, first aid kit, flare gun and other items into the tarp and then tied a rope to it so that he and his wife could drag it to the beach. He checked the radio and found that it still wasn't working, but the emergency beacon was still running, so he was relieved to be able to share this news with an already distraught wife waiting for him back in the trees.

Throughout the day, Ralph made a simple lean-to with pieces of driftwood washed up on the beach. He used the tarp as a roof and palm leaves as bedding for them to sleep on. He found coconuts laying around, which relieved his wife. Together with the remaining sandwiches and potato chips in the cooler, he figured they had enough food for another day, plenty of time for the coast guard to locate their boat. His wife had collected dead branches and pieces of driftwood along the beach for a fire. It took all day in the sun for the wood to dry out enough so that Ralph could start a fire. After the sun went down, Ralph found a packet of weatherproof matches in the first aid kit and made a fire, which helped calm his wife and lighten the mood.

"How many flares do we have?" she asked.

"Two, so we'll need to wait until we can either see a boat in the distance or hear a plane overhead. We don't want to waste them."

Why didn't the coast guard find us today?" she whined.

"I think we're one of many who need their help due to the storm," he assured her. "There are just so many of them to deal with all the calls they must have received throughout it. They'll get us by tomorrow, for sure. Look—you can see the red flashing of the boat's beacon from here. As long as that is on, it's just a matter of time before they find us."

"I sure hope you're right," he wife muttered.

Sometime during the night, Ralph was awakened by what sounded like a low growling noise coming from the jungle. He let his wife sleep and threw more wood onto the fire and took out the flare gun for protection. He could not sleep the rest of the night, and in the early morning, just before the sun came up, he noticed that the red flashing from the boat's beacon had stopped. At least for now, they were stranded.

When his wife woke up, they ate the remaining ham and cheese sandwich and a handful of potato chips. Having run out of water, they drank what they could from the coconuts.

Sensing his wife's dismay over the situation, he could not avoid the obvious.

"We can't continue to sit around here," Ralph told her. "We're out of food and water, and we have a couple of days—in this heat—before we start to get into real trouble. We need to go into the interior of island to find a water source."

"But what about the beacon!"

"It ran out of power during the early morning hours."

He decided to keep the growling he heard to himself for now; telling her would make their predicament much worse.

"But we still have the flares!"

"I know, but they won't do us any good until we can see or hear a plane or a boat. We only have two, as I told you, and we can't afford to waste them."

"This is all your fault, Ralph!" she shouted. "Why did I ever let you talk me into this stupid trip!"

He knew this was coming but ignored it. "Here," he said, passing her the medical kit.

"Wait a minute!" she yelled, throwing the medical kit to the ground. "What about the fishing rods? Can't we catch some fish?"

"We don't have any bait," he dryly answered her. "Besides, we can live longer without food, but in this heat, we can only survive three days without water. I filled our soda bottle with as much fluid as I could get from the coconuts, so if we conserve, we'll be OK for a day or two. After that, we will be in big trouble. We really need to get moving. I'll bring a rod with me in case we find some large insects or worms along the way, but our only objective now is to find a water source."

Beginning to cry, she picked up the medical kit, while Ralph carried the empty cooler, flare gun and fishing rod.

"This is all we need to bring with us," he said, tucking the flare gun into his belt. "Follow me."

Ralph and Zelma hiked through the jungle, but their progress was terribly slow without a machete to help clear a path. Ralph was especially alert from the growling he heard the night before, so he was glad he at least had the flare gun in case they came across some dangerous animal along the way.

"How do you know where to go?" his wife asked.

"I think that if we just climb upwards along the way, we'll reach some higher ground where we can get a better look at the island from above. Perhaps we'll see something of a village or even a town; we really have no idea how big or small this island is."

Her silence betrayed her faith in him.

A few hours later, they came upon a thin stream that emptied into a small basin. The water was clear, so he filled the empty water bottle with it, and they drank their fill. After a rest and filling the bottle and small cooler, they continued their hike up the gentle slope.

When they finally reached the highest point from where they started, they could see their boat and the beach where they spent their first night. They had a panoramic view of just over 180 degrees, but they couldn't see anything other than a dense jungle beneath their position, and there was a higher peak behind them blocking their view of the rest of the island. Seeing no settlements below, they had no choice but to climb to the next summit.

Once there, they could see that they were on a small island. They could also see two other islands in the distance. One was far away, but the other one was much closer, but still too far away to swim to. Exhausted and hungry, they decided to spend the night where they were. It also gave them a great vantage point from where to fire the flare gun if a plane or boat happened by.

The dead branches and leaves on the ground were too wet to make a fire, so they were going to have to spend the night in the light of the moon and stars. This weighed heavily on Zelma, and Ralph could not do or say anything to keep her from crying until after the sun disappeared.

Taking another look around before he laid down for the night, Ralph could hardly believe his eyes; there were lights coming from the nearby island! He showed his wife, and she started screaming for help.

"Shoot off the flare!" she said. "Shoot off the flare!"

Ralph hesitated to fire a flare, only having the two, but he figured it was worth the chance. If they returned a flare or some other optical response, then he would still have one left, so he fired it from the flare gun. Looking intently at the lights from the other island for a response, none came.

"Fire another one!" Zelma demanded. "Fire another one!"

"I can't, Zelma!" he yelled back. "It's the only one we have left."

"I don't care!" Can't you see the lights? Someone lives there! They'll see it this time!"

"I can't," Ralph insisted. "If they don't see it, then that's it, because we'll have no more left!"

"Gimmie that gun!" she demanded, reaching to take it from his hand.

"No Zelma!"

She fought with Ralph like a wild animal, and it took everything he had in his power to keep from striking her, yet she continued to attack him. Reaching to force the gun from his hand, she stumbled and fell down. When she tried to stand, she stumbled again, only this time she started to slip down the wet summit of leaves and mud until she rolled over and over down the slope and out of sight. Ralph carefully inched his way down after her, feeling terrible about the fight.

"Are you OK?" Ralph shouted out to her. She did not respond.

He wanted to fly down the slippery slope, but he had to be smart about it and inch his way along the muddy path without tumbling down himself.

When he finally reached his wife, she had just started to get on her knees.

"Are you OK?" he asked.

"Do I look 'OK,' Ralph! Look at what you did! What kind of man are you to push his wife down a mountain!"

"Honey, I didn't push you, you were trying to take away the gun and I couldn't let you have it . . . "

"You're not a man!" she interrupted. "In fact, you're not even half a man!" You are only good for two things, Ralph! Good for nothing and no good at all! Look at me! You're lucky I didn't break a leg! How are we gonna get out of this mess now! Just wait until I get my hands on you! I'm going to kill you, Ralph! D'ya hear me! I'm gonna ring your neck with my own two hands!"

At just that precise moment in the middle of her relentless tirade, something in the shape of a large man, but covered in fur, leapt on Ralph's wife, and began shredding her with its claws. Among her screams, Ralph pulled out the flare gun and pointed it at the creature, trembling in stark-raving terror. Suddenly the creature hesitated and looked up at Ralph.

"What are you waiting for!? Shoot it!" his wife pleaded.

As Ralph began to put pressure on the trigger, the creature slowly, yet deliberately, nodded its head side to side as if to say, "Don't do it."

Astonished, Ralph was about to pull the trigger when two more creatures crept out of the jungle.

"For God's sake, Ralph, what are you waiting for?" Zelma begged, her voice weakening.

The creature continued to penetrate Ralph's unbelieving eyes with its glare as if it were actually trying to communicate, "Don't do it, leave us be."

Realizing he only had one flare left against these three creatures, Ralph yielded to them by lowering his arm. As soon as the flare gun was at his side, they tore into his fat wife like sharks in a feeding frenzy. They wasted no time devouring her and as they ripped her to pieces with their claws and teeth, Ralph, no longer able to stand from the shock of it all, sat down in the mud. As he watched the grisly scene, an almost indiscernible grin began at the corner of his mouth until it reached the other side, and then he laughed. He was in shock, and he laughed like a madman while the creatures relentlessly tore at his wife, gorging on her. When they were finished, the first creature looked into Ralph's eyes one more time, almost with a glimpse of acknowledgement, and then they disappeared back into the jungle as quickly as when they first appeared.

Ralph sat in the same spot until the sunrise. As the brilliant streams of the morning sun shot through the jungle trees and vines, the condition of his wife became clearer with each passing minute. There wasn't much of her left. He did not dare venture further down to investigate, but he could plainly see they left very little of her behind. After the sun was higher in the sky, the gruesome scene became even more horrific. The creatures left the hands and feet intact, but they took her head with them, and he wondered why.

"Goodbye, Zelma," he said, apathetically.

"Here's the key to the boat," Val said, passing it to Keith. "Go ahead and start it up while Wheezer unties it from the dock.

With Keith, Janis and Val seated in the boat, Wheezer threw the rope to Keith, who caught it and then coiled it up before placing it neatly on the floor of the craft.

A moment later, the four of them were on their 20-minute boat ride to Neo, where Val had yet another "surprise" waiting for them.

As they got closer to the island, two large buildings began to appear through the morning mist.

"You see those structure on the beach?" Val pointed to.

"Yes," Keith and Janis both replied.

The building on the left is where I keep the wildest, the most dangerous of my animals. This is the group of animals that I draw from for my experiments back on the main island. The building on the right is where we are headed. This is where I keep the majority of my animals that have already responded successfully to my treatment. I can hardly wait to show them to you.

After docking the boat and tying it off, Keith and Wheezer assisted Val into a lightweight wheelchair already waiting for him under a canvas tarp on the dock.

As Keith pushed Val's wheelchair from behind toward the large building, Val said, "I am going to make a statement that will—no doubt—cause you both some discomfort. You may even think me mad in the twilight of my life, but I assure you, I am not.

"We scientists have developed a number of biochemical and genetic techniques by which DNA can be separated, rearranged, and transferred from one cell to another. Certain laboratory methods help us study the properties of genes in nature—for example, by comparing DNA from different animals to find out whether those animals are closely related to each other or as distant relatives only. Other DNA techniques provide tools for genetic engineering, the alteration of genes in an organism, for instance. These tools are used in the industry to develop commercial products, such as hardier crops, microbes that can break down oil slicks or decompose garbage and improve medicines.

"Janis, you are especially close to my work, and you should have reasoned with yourself by now why I have brought you into the intimacy of my home and work."

"I was sort of beginning to wonder what the purpose of your invitation was, Val," she said, walking beside him.

"You and I—we connect at a more scientific level, but it's cold logic that will partner us together. Sometimes, I wish we were, indeed, more like the animals, don't you?"

Val pressed his palm on the outdoor palm reader and the main door slid open, releasing a cacophony of animal sounds comprised mostly of apes and monkeys.

"I couldn't survive my cynicism if I didn't chase after my dreams," Val said. "Don't tell me I'm wrong either. Humankind would be happier, not when we cure male pattern baldness or devise a pill that improves our memory, but when we can attain a level of communication across all the races of the planet. Think how the world would benefit overall if everyone in it spoke the same language? More than this, what if we could speak to one another without language altogether and communicate with just our thoughts? No more confusion with what we are trying to say to each other when words so easily get lost in translation.

"I'm acquainted with your work, Janis," Val said. "Your work with autism has kept me extremely anxious for months in the hope that I could interest you in a visit to my home, where I could show you—not the unimaginable—but the unthinkable.

"Nothing can prepare you for what you are about to see, which is why I am dispensing with all the superfluous scientific background, for now. Once you see what I am going to show you, you will be amazed, shocked, and excited all at the same time. All my work will speak for itself! I am hoping that you will represent me to the universities throughout the states, Janis. The world as we know it today will be changed as quickly as it was with the automobile, the television, the internet, and the cell phone."

Val led them through another secure door, which opened up to a large room. Keith noted the cleanliness throughout and the absence of urine odor, which he was expecting with the abundance of animals nearby.

Val asked Wheezer to help transfer him into an electric wheelchair, and then he dismissed him to tend to the animals. He steered himself to a panel of buttons and switches, where he turned the lights on and increased the air conditioning. Fluorescent lights slowly blinked to life all along the high ceiling, exposing an operating table, expensive-looking medical equipment, animal cages, scores of cabinets, and a large Jacuzzi-like tub.

On one side of the room, there were double doors that obviously led to where the animals were kept. Val pressed the joystick on his wheelchair and crossed the room toward the double doors.

"Come with me," he beckoned to Keith and Janis. Joining him at the double doors, he told them to brace themselves for something really special, a once-in a lifetime experience.

When the doors slid open, there was an enormous adult chimpanzee in a dark brown jumper, sitting on a couch with its legs crossed. Keith was immediately intimidated by it since it was not confined in any manner. On an end table by the couch there was a lamp and a stack of books and magazines. On a coffee table in front of the couch there were a couple bunches of bananas and a large cup. On the left side of the room there was another door with a palm reader next to it. Keith wondered why the chimp was outside its cage, but he did not have to wonder for long.

"Keith . . . Janis . . . this is Diogenes, my favorite chimpanzee. He's quite a clever fellow, considering his age."

"How old is he?" Janis asked.

"He's twenty-seven, which is quite old for a chimp. Males live to be about thirty, though females tend to live a little longer, typically by five years."

"He's a magnificent specimen," Keith said.

"That he is, indeed!" Val said, raising his voice through an open smile.

"How did you come to select the name 'Diogenes'? Janis asked.

"That's a good and valid question, my dear," Val said, moving his wheelchair closer to the ape. "As you may, or may not know, Diogenes was one of the more obscure philosophers, perhaps one the greatest of the Cynical philosophers. Like this ape, Diogenes too, lived very simply. He lived in a wine barrel and owned only a cloak, a staff, and a bowl, until he caught a child drinking from it one day, which inspired him to throw it away in his pursuit of living as simply as possible, since he saw that his bowl still held value, even if it was from a young child's use of it. Similarly, this chimp does not own anything. All he requires is food and water. Anything on top of this is a treat, and don't get me wrong, he enjoys his treats, but he doesn't pursue them as humans pursue such things and all the other possessions they stockpile for themselves.

"Dio—that's what I call him—he is my success story."

Suddenly, the ape climbed off the couch and ambled with its wide, bowed legs to Val. It presented its hand to him in a gesture of acknowledgement and affection.

"You see? He knows me and trusts me. Apes at this age tend to be very unpredictable and violent, but not Dio, and do you want to know why?"

"You've been giving him your formula," Janis ventured a guess.

"Indeed," Val responded proudly. "It was with Dio that I perfected my formula. Additionally, in order to maintain his contented, tame, and loving temperament, I have been able to reduce injections to every three days. In fact, he is due for one this morning, and I cannot be late; there is a short window of time before the effects begin to wear off. The real challenge now is to reduce it to a single injection for the entire life of the animal.

"Watch this. Dio, fetch me a banana."

The ape tilted its head as if to concentrate on the words, and then it turned around, grabbed a banana from the coffee table and returned to Val with it.

"Amazing," Janis remarked.

"How much is one plus two?" Val asked the Chimp.

Without hesitation the ape held up three fingers.

"I can't believe what I am seeing!" Keith laughed with astonishment.

The chimp turned his attention to Keith and in perfect diction said, "Your laugh could peel the paint off of furniture."

Exhausted, starving, and almost in a state of shock, Ralph continued to push himself down the other side of the highest peak on the island, having left what remained of his wife to the flies and worms. He could not figure out in his tired mind what those three things were that attacked and then devoured her, practically whole... They weren't monkeys or apes, they were almost man-like, but certainly not men. Covered in short hair with claws on their humanoid hands, and those eyes... there was an intelligence about them. The leader of the pack somehow communicated with him, warning Ralph to back off, to not interfere, and then they left him alone to escape. He couldn't think straight. None of the horrible episode made any sense.

As he came closer to the beach, and much to his surprise and good fortune, Ralph spotted what appeared to be a large house in the distance. In fact, as he got closer, there were, indeed, two houses. He was saved, he thought.

"Hello!" he shouted just above a whisper, having lost his strength to even scream. When he was several feet from one of the structures, he slowed down his pace when he noticed a boat tied to a dock. He truly was saved, he thought. Soon he would have water and some food and then he could contact the coast guard—surely, they had a radio.

Suddenly his excitement for salvation was displaced by the image of his wife laying on her back in a pool of blood with her ribs exposed and with her head missing... how would he explain this?

Keith and Janis stood with their jaws hanging in disbelief. Val appeared to enjoy the shock he gave them and let the reality of what they just witnessed sink in.

"He talks," Janis gushed. "I heard him; he spoke!"

Val dismissed the chimp, who took the bananas on his way to another door off the room. Keith was still momentarily baffled.

"Of course, he talks!" Val said triumphantly.

"I don't understand," Keith said, finding his tongue. "How is this possible? Did you somehow teach him to speak? Is this an elaborate trick?"

"He reasons, Keith!"

"Your formula . . . it reduces aggression . . . it can make an animal talk . . . but how is it possible that it can also give it a soul?"

"Why would you believe that animals do not have a soul? Of course, they do. Take a dog, for instance. When he is misbehaving and you discipline him, doesn't he react like a child to the scolding? When you pat him and cover him with praise, doesn't he react in pure love—as a child would? I'm not saying all animals have souls . . . crocodiles and sharks are more like machines, but consider the elephant, dolphin, and ape. We already know there are levels of intelligence in animals—with the apes being our closest relatives. All my formula does is unlock a larger percentage of their brain's capability to free up the part of it that allows reasoning and the ability to communicate. If animals could have the capacity to reason, then they could choose between reacting with less aggression—love, even—or continue to be wild. So far, all of my animals opt for acceptance and affection, which is clearly one of the results—or side effects if you wish—of my formula. With a few adjustments I recently made to my formula, it permits certain animals, like the apes, to reason, and if they can reason, then they can communicate, and since the anatomy of a chimp's mouth is close to a human's, they can even articulate words!

"This is all my formula does—it opens closed doors, and then the rest is up to us to educate and nurture, such as what I did by teaching Dio to speak and to behave in a civilized manner. Not every animal treated with my formula will have the same result: a dog does not have the physiological capability of forming words with the shape of its mouth as a chimp does. The point I am making is that apes are the closest to humans in terms of intelligence, physiology, and anatomy. They can never be fully human, of course, since they are apes, but with training and education, the possibilities are endless."

"I suppose it's just too much to process all at once, Val," Janis said, sitting down on the couch.

"I understand," Val said. "Now that you two are settled down, are you ready for the "surprise?"

"I thought Dio was your surprise," Keith said, sitting down next to his wife.

Val pressed a button on a console next to the couch, and the door that Dio exited through a moment before slid open. In a moment, Dio returned holding the hand of a young chimpanzee as it walked beside him.

"This is the surprise," Val said, taking the chimp from Dio.

I named her Modern. She's just learning to speak, herself.

"You've been injecting her with your formula too?" Janis asked.

"No, and here's the surprise: she was born with the capacity to reason and speak on her own without the injections! She is the daughter of Dio and a wild chimpanzee! Modern is the beginning of an entirely new race, equal to man in every way aside from anatomy!"

Suddenly, a siren went off.

"What's going on?" Keith said, standing to his feet.

"I don't know, Val replied, handing Modern back into Dio's arms, and instructing them to return to their quarters.

"Follow me," Val told Keith and Janis, leading them to another door off the room.

"This is my control room, similar to the one back at the main house," Val said, as he switched on the lights and brought the monitors to life.

"Look!" Janis exclaimed. "There's a man outside!"

Val could not believe his eyes. Neo Island was set up to be so secure that no one from the outside world would ever be able to step foot on it and then live to tell about it. He had the apes of his experimental failures patrolling the entire island, always on the prowl for fresh meat, on top of what Wheezer already provided them with. There were only two of them remaining, but the island was small enough for them to deal with trespassers.

"He's at the door, Val, look!" Keith exclaimed, pointing at the monitor.

"We better let him in, Doctor," Janis demanded.

When Ralph knocked on the main outside door, Val buzzed him in.

"Go get him, Keith," Val insisted. Janis and I will meet you in the main room. I'll leave the doors open for you.

Keith complied and ran to meet Ralph at the outside door. When Ralph saw Keith, he fell to his knees from complete exhaustion and thanked God for getting him to safety.

"Where did you come from?" Keith implored. "How did you even get here?"

"My wife and I got trapped in a storm," he panted. "On vacation . . . ended up on the other side of the island . . . please, let me have some water."

"Of course," Keith said, helping Ralph to his feet and into the building. By then, Janis, Val and Wheezer were there to meet the stranger.

"Wheezer, fetch this man some food and water.

"Bring him into the main room, Keith," Val said, leading the way.

Wheezer soon returned with a tray of bottled water, fruit, and cold chicken. After guzzling the water and eating some of the chicken, Ralph looked around the room, and returning his gaze upon the others, he broke down and cried.

"It must have been an awful experience," Janis said, placing her hand on Ralph's shoulder.

"I wouldn't even know how to begin," Ralph said, wiping his tears. "I came with my wife."

"Where is she?" Keith asked, handing him his handkerchief.

"She's dead," Ralph said, composing himself. "We were attacked last night . . . by these animals . . . unlike anything I've ever seen."

"What did they look like?" Val asked, knowing full well what they were.

"There were three of them . . . "

"Three?" Val echoed. "You say three? Are you certain there were three of them?"

"Yes, I'm certain!" Ralph shouted, "I was there, I watched them devour my wife before my very eyes!"

"Yet they left you alone?" Keith asked.

"I know, I don't understand it," Ralph replied. "But they weren't like any animals I've ever seen. They were more human than they were animal . . . in shape, I mean . . . perhaps, even in intelligence . . . I just don't know what to think . . . "

Val patiently listened.

"What did they look like," Janis asked.

"Well, they could have been monkeys, or apes, you know, like gorillas, but they weren't gorillas. The one thing I saw that I still cannot figure out, is that their hands . . . they weren't like the paws of an animal or like the hands of an ape . . . they were human-like, except they had long claws on them. When I initially tried to reach my wife, one of them looked up to me and . . . " Ralph paused, trying to find the words.

"Yes?" Janis asked impatiently.

"He looked straight at me and shook his head as if to say "no," warning me in a way that meant that I'd better stay where I was. When they finished, they ran back into the jungle as quickly as they came at my wife. My wife is still up there. We need to go get her body!"

"It's far too dangerous," Val interrupted.

"What are we supposed to do, then? Just leave her there?"

"Absolutely not," Val replied. "I will send my man up there to retrieve her. He's a professional hunter and will be well armed. By the way, you said you saw three of them. Are you certain you saw three?"

"Yes! I saw three! I watched all three of these things maul my wife to death in front of my eyes and then they ate her!

"I apologize, sir," Val said, his response coldly unsympathetic.

Val faced a dilemma. What began as a wonderful day with his introduction of Dio and Modern to Keith and Janis was fragmenting into a disaster, one that he was beginning to think he would never be able to recover from without taking drastic measures. Certainly, he could not let Ralph leave the island only to share his story with the press once he returned to the mainland. There would be an investigation on the island. There would be police and reporters and then they would be followed by all sorts of curious busy bodies, with all of his work up in smoke. He would have to ponder on options before taking any action.

As Ralph continued to share more details of his ordeal with Keith and Janis, Val continued to be perplexed by Ralph's sighting of three apes instead of the two that he himself released into the jungles of the island. The other confusing detail from Ralph's account is that they did not seem to be his apes at all. There is an obvious difference between a chimpanzee and a man, yet he kept repeating that he saw humanoid-shaped creatures. What were these? What happened to his two apes? There were too many questions without answers, and he needed time to figure out what was going on before anyone contacted the mainland.

There was also Dio and Modern to think about.

He was confident that Keith and Janis would keep everything to themselves, but what was he going to do to protect Dio and Modern from the authorities, not to mention his competitors and others? He needed time to think.

"I believe everyone could use a drink," Val suggested.

"Good idea," Keith responded. "I know I could use one."

Val wheeled himself to the kitchen and found a bottle of brandy. He went to a drawer hidden beside the dishwasher and retrieved a small brown bottle with a white powder in it. He tapped some of it into each of the three glasses and filled them to the brim with the brandy.

Returning to the main room with the tray of drinks on his lap, he offered each of them a glass. Ralph greedily gulped his down at once, while Keith and Janis sipped theirs. Moments later, Ralph passed out.

"The poor man is totally spent," Janis said.

"Keith, bring him to my bedroom; it's off the kitchen. Let him rest and we'll call the coast guard."

Keith and Janis complied and carried Ralph to Val's bedroom and put him into bed, removing is shoes.

"I'm actually feeling a little wiped out myself," Keith shared with his wife.

"Funny . . . I do too."

Within moments, both Keith and Janis passed out from the drug Val slipped into their drinks. As soon as he confirmed all three were out cold, he gave instructions to Wheezer to take Dio into the jungle at the usual spot where they left meat intended for the two roaming apes.

"That intruder is delusional from a lack of food and water," Val said. Only Hansel and Gretel have free reign of the island. There aren't three of them. You and Dio are to hide and wait for them to show up for their meat at the usual place, and then you are to shoot them and bury the evidence. I can't have them on the island if there's the possibility of a breach."

"Why do we need to destroy them? Can't we put them is cages until this blows over?"

"They are now man-eaters, Wheezer. They must be destroyed, and I want it done before the sedative I gave Janis, Keith and the other man wears off. The castaway needs to be kept out of my sight."

Later in the afternoon, five creatures emerged cautiously from the jungle. It was obvious that two of them were the experimental apes, Hansel and Gretel, but Wheezer had no account for the other three that walked on two legs like men. Together, they all approached the table of meat cautiously.

"I thought I ordered you to kill Hansel and Gretel," Wheezer whispered angrily to Dio.

"I only killed Hansel," Dio retorted, "in fact, I hacked him into pieces with an ax and buried him four feet in the ground! I wasn't able to find Gretel. Besides, where did the other three come from?"

"Obviously, you did not kill Hansel, Dio! He's right there!"

"Then what did I kill and bury last week?"

"Perhaps it was one of the other things, but it wasn't Hansel or Gretel."

Wheezer and Dio pulled their rifles from their shoulders and quietly placed the barrels of them on the large rock they were hiding behind.

"When they're in the middle of feeding, and when I give the word, start firing," Wheezer commanded. "This time, make sure they are all dead—you understand?"

"Yes," Dio complied, aiming his rifle at the group.

While the two apes and three other creatures were gorging themselves on the meat left for them, Wheezer gave the command and he and Dio shot and killed all five. Walking through the brush, they approached them, and as he surmised, the apes were Hansel and Gretel.

"See?" Wheezer said, pointing at them on the bloody ground. "I don't know who or what your got rid of, but it wasn't either of these two."

"But where did the other three come from?" Dio asked, confused.

"I don't know, perhaps there was a forth. I'll take one of them back to the doctor. You get busy and bury the rest of them. I'll be back to help you."

"Alright," Dio acknowledged with a heavy sigh.

When Wheezer brought Val to the back room of the building, he explained how there were indeed, three more creatures along with Hansel and Gretel, but they did not look like anything he had ever seen.

Wheezer lifted the creature up onto a stainless-steel table and slid Val's wheelchair into a lift so that he could navigate himself around it for a better look.

"I should have sterilized the apes," Val said despondently. "This is one of their offspring."

"Offspring?"

"There's no other explanation. The failure of the formula to work on Hansel and Gretel obviously had other side-effects I never considered. You can clearly see the resemblance to an ape in its face, but the eyes are narrower and set further apart. The castaway—Ralph, is his name—he mentioned that one of these creatures seemed to demonstrate a degree of intelligence. Firstly, it gestured for Ralph to stay away while he and the other two attacked his wife. Secondly, it didn't attack Ralph, and thirdly, as perhaps their leader, it kept the other two from attacking him."

"Do you think we got all of them? There was a forth one—the one that Dio got rid of. He thought it was Hansel, but it was one of these things."

"I believe so, since all of them came for the meat at the same time ... like a family, my God. If there were others, they certainly would have come for the meat as well."

"It's only been a matter of months since we released Hansel and Gretel back into the wild," Wheezer said. "If these things are their offspring, how could they have grown so quickly?"

"Obviously, yet another adverse side effect of my earlier recipe of the formula. My recent versions of the formula appear to have resolved whatever it was in the proteins that caused the birth and accelerated growth of these monstrosities.

"Where's Dio now?"

"He's getting rid of them, like you wanted. I should get back and help him bury them."

"Yes," Val said, drifting off in his thoughts.

"What about this one?" Wheezer asked.

"When you and Dio finish up, get back here and help me destroy it by throwing it into the incinerator."

"Yes, Doctor," Wheezer complied, and then he was gone.

Val returned to the main room and waited for Keith and Janis to wake up. This gave him time to think of a way to murder Keith, Janis, and Ralph. He would need to find Ralph's boat on the other side of the island and sink it in the ocean. He would also need to get rid of any trace of Keith's and Janis's visit to his islands. After about an hour, he heard someone walking toward the main room.

Dio

Stumbling into the main room with his hand to his head, Keith fell back into the couch.

"I must have fallen asleep," Keith said, rubbing his face.

"All of you have been through a lot today," Val said, lighting a cigar. "How are Janis and Ralph?"

"Ralph is still asleep, but Janis will be out after she finishes washing up. I'm sorry, Doc, I don't know what came over us so suddenly. I guess we just needed to crash for a while. Where's Dio and Modern?"

Blowing a thick cloud of smoke overhead, Val answered, "He's in the other building doing his chores: feeding the animals and cleaning out their cages. Modern is taking her nap. After we've had something to eat, I'll have Dio join us. You'll be amazed by what he's learned already."

"When I woke up, I thought I must have been having a dream, but apparently, this is no dream," Keith said, shaking his head.

Janis entered the main room and apologized for falling asleep on her host, but Val interrupted her and told her not to think of it, that it was perfectly understandable, considering all of the excitement that transpired over the last few hours.

"I think Ralph is waking up too," she said. "I imagine he'll join us in a short while."

While Val, Keith and Janis discussed the possibilities of the formula, as well as what Keith thought were potential, adverse consequences regarding integration of speaking, thinking apes into society, Wheezer and Dio were already busy with destroying the creature in the back room by burning the evidence. When they finished, they washed up, changed clothes, and while Dio went to the other building to check on the animals, Wheezer entered the main room.

"Oh, by the way, did you get in touch with the coast guard?" Val asked him.

"Yes doctor," Wheezer lied, "they are on their way. ETA is about 90 minutes."

This meant that Val had less than 90 minutes to get rid of his two visitors and the castaway before they started asking about the coast guard again when they were never going to show up.

"We'll go back to the main island and wait for the coast guard. I don't want anyone snooping around here," Val said, "but first, I need to give Dio his injection; it is way overdue. While I'm taking care of this, please make yourselves comfortable. There is plenty of food in the refrigerator, and an assortment of crackers and cookies are in the cabinet next to it. Help yourself to anything you want to drink."

When Val entered the back room, he was pleased to see it was already cleaned up. He wheeled over to the incinerator and raised the temperature to ensure nothing remained of the creature, including the bones.

"I need to give Dio his injection," Val said, turning around to face another refrigerator. I'm afraid with everything that's been going on today, I am very late with his shot. Go next door and bring him to me."

Wheezer left Val, preparing a syringe.

When Wheezer walked into the building, the animals were acting excited: the apes were rattling their cages and the big cats were circling themselves in their enclosed habitats. Wheezer called out to Dio, but he did not answer. Over in a far corner of the confinement area, he saw that Modern was also behaving erratically, hiding under a blanket.

"Dio!" Wheezer called out, but again, no response.

He wasn't taking any chances, so he pulled out a pistol from a drawer and started searching the building. Not being able to locate Dio, he assumed he might have returned to the lab next door for his injection.

Suddenly, Wheezer felt an incredible pain in his chest. Looking down, he saw an iron rod broken off from a cage protruding out of his chest. He dropped the gun and wrapped his hands around the rod in disbelief. He turned around and saw Dio just standing there with a wild expression on his face. A large amount of blood was all around his mouth and dripping on his chest.

"Dio," Wheezer gasped, "what have you done?"

Falling to his knees, Wheezer reached for the pistol, but Dio rushed at Wheezer and twisted his head off, throwing it into the tiger's enclosure, where it attracted two tigers in claiming the prize.

By now Ralph had joined the others and was enjoying gouda and crackers with a can of ginger ale. While still waking up, a loud sound came from the back room off of the main room.

"What was that?" Janis shouted.

"I don't know, but let's go find out," Keith suggested.

Entering the back room, they saw Dio had just jammed a large syringe through Val's remaining eye, all the way into his brain. He turned around to face the three shocked individuals, with the door having just slid closed behind them.

Without any time to think, Keith scanned the lab and opened a cabinet to his side, hoping for anything he could use as a weapon. Much to his astonishment, it was lined with rifles and other firearms. He snatched one from the middle of the rack and hoped against hope that it was loaded.

Pointing the rifle at Dio, he said, "What is going on, Dio? What have you done to the doctor? Stay where you are, or I'll shoot!"

Dio hesitated his advance toward the frightened trio, and narrowing his eyes, he focused on Keith. There was no longer any sign of the gentleness and intelligence he had earlier demonstrated. With a blood-curdling shriek, Dio jumped at Keith. Without any reluctance, Keith pulled the trigger of the rifle and was overwhelmingly relieved when it fired a bullet into Dio's heart, shooting him dead.

Janis rushed over to check on Val, but he was dead too.

"Wheezer!" Keith called out, but there was no answer. "Ralph, take this gun and go see if Wheezer is in the next room, but be careful."

After a couple of minutes, Ralph shouted from the other room that Wheezer was dead, as well. "But don't come in!" he warned.

"What now?" Janis sobbed, no longer able to withhold her distress over all that just occurred.

"We need to burn everything down to the ground," Ralph demanded. "Nothing but evil can come out of this place."

"I agree," Keith replied.

"What about Modern?" Janis implored the men.

"Modern . . . " Keith nodded. "We can't leave her here; we'll take her with us."

"Nothing can leave the premises," Ralph insisted.

"So, we're just going to murder her?" Janis asked angrily.

"Think of what you're suggesting," Ralph argued. "You'll be responsible for introducing this madman's creation into the world!"

"I'm sorry, Ralph," Keith said firmly, "she's more human than she is ape. She leaves with us, and we'll deal with it later. You two get to the boat and once you are safely in it, I'll release the animals and then burn everything else to the ground."

Ralph and Janis ran to the boat with Janis holding Modern close to her chest. Once settled in the boat, Ralph started the engine.

Fifteen minutes later, Keith came bolting for the dock before any of the wild animals he released had a chance to meet with him along the way. The only things he brought with him was a rifle and a small duffle bag, which further irritated Ralph, believing Keith was saving the doctor's notes and journals, but he was outnumbered. Defeated, he slumped in the captain's chair, waiting for Keith to untie the boat from the dock and jump aboard.

Within minutes as they started back for the main island, the two buildings on Neo were fully ablaze, followed shortly by two explosions: propane tanks and cannisters of gasoline, and many other flammables, no doubt.

"Why hasn't the coast guard arrived yet?" Janis shouted over the roar of the boat.

"They lied to us," Keith said, stating the obvious.

When they docked at the main island, they made their way to the house.

"Hold on," Janis said, stopping in her tracks. "How are we going to get into the house? We don't have any keys, and remember the palm readers? Only Val and Wheezer had access to them.

Keith opened the bag and pulled out Val's severed right hand.

"It's a good thing I remembered too," he said, putting it back. "I cut it off before letting the animals out.

"What is happening to us?" Ralph groaned, shaking his head. "We need to get back to the mainland . . . I'm losing my mind."

"We will, Ralph," Keith assured him. "We just need to get some food and water and a few other things before we get going. Fill up the boat with gas and fill a couple more cannisters for the trip. I'll contact the coast guard to let them know we are on our way."

Just then, another explosion was faintly heard in the distance.

"I guess I know why Val named his creation, 'Dio,'" Keith said, turning around to face the fires on the island.

"How's that?" Janis asked.

"Ironically, it was Plato who described Diogenes as, 'A Socrates gone mad.'"

Where Do Flies Go at Night?

"You're such an animal," she said, playfully struggling out of his hold from behind.

"What?" he teased.

"C'mon, let me go, and wash up for dinner. We're having streak tonight."

"How can we afford steak?" he asked, with genuine interest.

"I saved money on our groceries by using coupons from Sunday's paper."

"That's my girl! I'll be back in a few minutes."

"Hurry up though; I know you like yours rare."

Wayne and Alison Haskell were still newlyweds, having married just less than a year ago. He worked at a night club as the assistant manager to Harry Ingles, owner of "The Lizard Lounge" in Boston, Massachusetts. Alison was a secretary for a law firm until she became pregnant six months ago when she resigned to become a full-time homemaker and soon-to-be mother. They moved into a run-down part of the neighborhood, but their apartment was clean and cheap. He was saving money for a small fixer-upper in the suburbs, but until then, they made their place comfortable with the nice furniture her parents gave them as a wedding gift.

The summer had been especially humid, and not able to afford an air-conditioner, they kept all the windows open to help get some air into the place. Unfortunately, this invited a lot of flies, moths, and mosquitoes into the place, especially the kitchen, so Alison had plenty of bug repellent and fly traps strategically placed throughout the apartment to help keep the infestation to a minimum. It was a double-edged sword, so to speak: if she closed the windows, there would be fewer flies, but the humidity would be unbearable, especially at night, when they couldn't sleep.

As her husband was washing up, she saw a fly buzzing around his steak. Having gained experience over the summer in swatting flies, she crept up on it and smashed it flat as a pancake on the countertop.

"Got 'cha!" she said, triumphantly.

"Got what?" Wayne asked, walking into the kitchen.

"Oh, I just killed another fly," she replied, flicking it from the swatter into the garbage can.

"Nice going, Sweetheart," he said, reaching for a couple of glasses from the cupboard.

"What's there to drink with dinner? What goes good with streak and baked potato?"

"I'm afraid all we have is some iced tea that I brewed this morning and some ginger ale. I'll have the iced tea, myself."

"Me too."

Wayne pulled out the iced tea carafe from the refrigerator and then got the ice tray from the freezer. "Sugar?"

Alison wiped her hands on her hips, threw her arms around his neck and gave him a big kiss.

"That's really nice, dear, but I meant sugar for the tea."

They both laughed.

"That was cute, honey. How was work today?" she asked, returning to the stove.

"Same 'ol, same 'ol," he said, pouring iced tea into their glasses. We had a customer—sort of a weird one, even for our neighborhood, come in before Happy Hour. I'd never seen her before, and believe me, I would never have forgotten a character like this if I had. She was dressed up in what I'd call gypsy clothes. With all of the weird fashions these days, with the colored hair, piercings, and tattoos, she sort of fit right in with the crowd except she didn't order anything. She sat at the far end of the bar sort of in her own little world. Later, when I was getting ready to come home, one of the bartenders came up to me with a book and said that he found it laying on the bar. When I went out to take a look around, she was gone. The bartender said he found it right where she was sitting, so I assumed she forgot it. I checked it out, but there isn't a name, address, or anything in it, so when I was about to put it into the Lost and Found box, I skimmed through it and found it pretty interesting. I probably shouldn't have brought it home with me, but I want to get a better look at it. It looks like a book of spells; witchcraft, maybe."

"Can I see it?"

"Sure, I'll get it from the car after dinner when I take out the garbage."

The next morning, Wayne walked into the manager's office to begin his shift. A young, attractive woman was standing next to his desk, waiting for him.

"Have you told her yet?" she asked.

"Not yet," Wayne answered the gorgeous bartender.

"Why not? You said you were going to tell her last night!"

"I intended to, but it wasn't the right time. I was late for dinner, and she went to bed early. She was feeling sick—I think from the pregnancy."

"I don't care, Wayne," she retorted. "You always seem to have an excuse. Do you want to be with me or not?"

"I do darling, believe me, I do! I just need to find the right time when I can sit her down and explain the situation."

"The 'situation'? What's that supposed to mean?"

"Try not to get all riled up, Mona. You know what I mean."

"I'm not so sure I do anymore, Wayne. Do you love me?"

"You know I love you."

"Then what is standing in the way? If you love me and if you want to be with me, then you would handle this like an adult and get it over with. I am not going to hang out on the hooks forever. In fact, if you do not take care of this by tomorrow, then we're through. Do you hear me? I mean it!"

"Yes, I hear you. Don't worry babe, I'll take care of it tonight for sure."

"You better, Wayne, or you and I are done. You understand?"

"Yes darling, I get it. Now give daddy some sugar."

The next morning, Alison let her husband sleep in since it was Saturday. She gathered his clothes from the bedroom floor and threw them into the hamper. She made herself a cup of coffee, and noticed the strange book left on the kitchen counter from the night before. It had an old, worn leather cover and there was a kind of symbol etched into it. She picked it up and immediately, a wave of nausea swept over her. The pregnancy had been difficult so far with morning sickness, with headaches throughout the day being the biggest challenges to deal with, but she was not concerned because in three short months she was going to be a mother with a new baby, and she couldn't wait.

She picked up the book and flipped through the pages. As a former secretary, she knew paper, and these pages were incredibly old, faded, and thick. She turned the book over to look at the back cover to see if there was an author or a publishing house or any other kind of identifier. Just like Wayne mentioned, there was no writing anywhere in the book to indicate whom it belonged to. She knew he would need to take it back to work with him on Monday in case the owner came looking for it, but in the meantime, she planned to spend the morning reading through it.

By noon, Wayne was up and asking for breakfast. As she made a cheese and onion omelet for him, she told him how interesting the book was. Apparently, it was a book of spells, and judging by the condition of the book, she surmised it could possibly be traced back to the Salem witch trials of early 1692.

"How do you figure that?" he yawned, pouring a cup of coffee.

"There is a reference to them in the middle of the book. It's almost written like a first-person account, as though the person who wrote it was actually there. You know me, I love stuff like this: horror stories, thrillers, mysteries . . . but this isn't a book of stories. It reads more like a diary, but throughout the book there are these spells, or recipes. For instance, here's one on how to walk among a crowd of people while being invisible . . .

"It's just a bunch a nonsense, Alison. If you saw the woman I saw yesterday, you would think she was a homeless person just coming into the bar to cool off from the heat outside. Besides, I'm not 100% sure it was even her who left this book behind. It could have been someone else, we just have no idea of knowing, right?"

"Well, all I can say is that this is a really cool book and I wish we could keep it."

"You can keep it," he said sipping is coffee.

"I can?" she chirped.

"Yeah, after 30 days if no one claims it, it's yours."

"Very funny, Wayne," she said, sarcastically. "Anyway, at least I have today and tomorrow to look through it before you have to bring it back."

"Sounds great, honey. This will give you something to do while I'm out golfing with Steve and Kevin."

"Oh, that's right, I almost forgot but it's OK since I have the laundry and some other housework to catch up on. Have a great day golfing, hon."

After Wayne left for the day, Alison could not wait to read through the book. After an hour, she decided to copy down several spells, such as the ones describing how to afflict an enemy with a disease or perpetual hiccups. She found herself giggling as many of the spells seemed so petty. Almost all of them seemed like recipes for revenge, such as afflicting a problem neighbor with a poor harvest or giving a jilted lover an untreatable rash.

She copied a dozen of them into her notebook and hid it under their mattress where Wayne would never look, but she was hopeful to make the book her own in a month if no one reclaimed it. A book this old had to be worth quite a bit of money to the right collector, she thought, and they could certainly use the money with a new baby on the way.

Later in the day, while Alison was sorting the laundry, she noticed a red smear on one of her husband's shirts. Upon closer inspection, the evidence did not lie. It was obviously lipstick, and it certainly was not hers since she doesn't use it. She also noted a small cloud of flies buzzing around the house, but she had no time for this. She was too hurt and angry to think about anything else.

When Wayne came home around dinnertime, she was ready and waiting with his shirt on her lap to show him. She wanted an explanation, and it had better be a good one. However, when she showed him the lipstick stain on the collar of his shirt, she could immediately tell in his expression that he had been unfaithful to her.

"How could you do this to me?" she sobbed. "How could you do this to *us*? We have a *baby* coming . . . we haven't even been married a full year yet . . . why would you need someone else if you love me . . . " All of these arguments fell out of her mouth in quick succession without giving him a chance to respond because how else could he answer her other than to admit he was caught seeing another woman.

Wayne did not respond. He did not know what to say because she was right. He had been behaving as he did before he met Alison, sleeping around with any woman he wanted to, but they never meant anything to him. He loved Alison.

She threw the shirt into his face and went into the bedroom to pack.

"I don't love her," he said, as she whirled around the bedroom like a tornado, throwing her clothes into a suitcase.

"I don't care if you love her or not!" she cried. "what difference does that make!"

"The difference is that I love you," he pleaded. "She's nothing to me. I'll end it now. I'll never see her again."

"Wayne, I don't care how you handle her. I only know that I never want to see you again. I'm going to move in with my parents. We're getting a divorce. There is no way I am going to go bring a baby into a marriage of convenience so that you can sleep around with whoever you want, whenever you want. I can no longer trust you! You are dead to me, Wayne!"

In the heat of the moment, Wayne knew there was nothing he could say to change her mind, so he left the bedroom and sat down on the couch in their living room, hoping he would have another chance to talk to her when she was calm. He did love her, and he knew that he had been behaving selfishly. He did not want to lose her, especially over some bartender, regardless of how beautiful she was. He knew that he had a life and a future with Alison. He bowed his head in shame as she said 'good-bye' before slamming the apartment door behind her.

As Wayne nursed his regrets with a bottle of scotch, he noticed that flies suddenly assailed the apartment. The more he swatted, the more they seemed to multiply until he had enough of it and sprayed insect pesticide throughout the house and closed all the windows. Perhaps he would die from the fumes, he thought, and perhaps that wouldn't actually be a bad thing, especially since he was feeling like a maggot himself.

Alison did not return any of his calls over the weekend, and here it was already Monday morning—time to face the music with Mona once and for all. As he walked past the kitchen counter, his eye caught a glimpse of the wretched spell book that Alison must have left for him to return, so he picked it up and threw it into his shoulder bag on his way out the door. The gypsy would likely return for it, he thought. Who else would possess a book as weird as this one?

After work, Mona came into the manager's office where Wayne was working on the inventory and wanted to know what was going on. He told her that he still loved his wife and that he was deeply sorry for leading her on for so long. Naturally, she did not take this well and quit on the spot, throwing her apron into his face.

When Wayne returned to the lonely apartment, he sat down on the couch with a bottle of bourbon he stole from the bar and drank himself into a stupor. He already missed his wife terribly. He cried into his hands, barely believing all that transpired over the last 24 hours.

Suddenly he realized something was different.

He lifted his wet face from his hands and looked around the room and noticed that there weren't any flies buzzing around. He left the windows open before he left for work, and they were all still wide open, but there wasn't a single fly in the entire apartment. "Perhaps that pesticide is the ticket," he thought.

He sat back into the couch, and while searching for the remote in the cushions, he noticed that a shiny black spider had made a large web in the far corner of his living room. Surprisingly, there appeared to be hundreds of flies trapped in it. He walked over to the web for a closer look of the spider. It was jet black with a tiny red spot on its abdomen.

Not realizing it was a deadly black widow, he slurred, "That's my girl. You can stay here as long as you earn your keep."

Reaching for the bottle from the coffee table to pour himself another drink, his doorbell rang. He instantly leapt to his feet thinking it was Alison returning to work things out. He put the glass down on the coffee table, ran his fingers through his hair, rushed to the door, and opened it wide only to see Mona standing in the hallway.

"What are you doing here?" he drawled, lowering his head in disappointment.

"I heard your wife left you. I'm sorry, Wayne, but you have to know that I still love you."

Wayne turned back to the living room to get his glass.

"I know this seems inappropriate, considering the situation with your wife, but I'm here for you Wayne. I love you."

Wayne remained silent, lost in regret and remorse over the loss of his wife. Mona closed the apartment door behind her and walked into the kitchen. Suddenly, a large, shiny black spider scampered across the kitchen floor toward her. Without hesitation, Mona stomped on it, squashing it to death.

Though things were never going to work out between Wayne and Mona, he never heard from his wife again.

All That Glitters

"What a particularly cold night," the old man said, throwing another log into the fireplace, vigorously rubbing his hands together before the hearth. His wife sat on her horsehair armchair, with a thick, wool blanket covering her shivering legs. She was 10 years his senior, and in recent years, she had become distant—fewer smiles and less intimate embraces for her long-suffering husband, especially since the love of her life, their only son, Wesley, mysteriously disappeared twenty years ago.

"Husband," she sighed, "put more wood on the fire."

He obeyed without speaking a word but shook his head in silent despair. Wood was becoming more difficult to harvest during the relentless string of snowstorms that assailed their tiny cabin. The season of trapping the past year was unfavorable. On top of this, much of their autumn storage of corn, apples and potatoes was already consumed, and for the rest of the village, it hadn't been much better.

As he reclined back into his Morris chair close to the fire, wondering what to do about the shortage of game out in the frost covered forest, a knock came upon the door.

"Why would anyone be out this late at night, and in this dreadful weather?" his wife asked, wearily.

He raised his tired body out of the comfort of his warm chair and took the six or seven steps to the cabin's heavy oak door.

"Who's there?" he asked.

"A friend," the tired voice answered. "Open the door and let me in."

"What do you want?" the old man asked, his heart beginning to pound nervously in his chest.

"I need food and shelter for the night."

"We have no food for you," he replied abruptly, "and we have no room for you, either."

"I was told down in the village that of all places, you—of all people—would be willing to provide some bread and a place on the floor before your fire. I'm exhausted from my travels, and I can pay my way."

All That Glitters

The old woman's eyes opened wide before the fire and suddenly the brilliance of the light flooded the room. Her entire countenance changed. She threw the blanket from her legs, stood up and rushed over to the door, pushing her daunted husband out of the way. "Come in! Come in!" she said, opening the heavy oak door against the falling snow outside. "We don't have much to offer, but all are welcome, so come inside. It is very cold, and we have a warm fire, and I will get you a warm drink. So, come in! Come in!"

Removing his badger mittens, the road-weary traveler came inside and sat in the Morris chair, warming his frozen hands before the fire.

"I apologize for being suspicious at first," the old man said, coughing, "but times are so hard these days, that there are thieves willing to kill for a mere morsel of food . . . one cannot be careful enough, if you understand my meaning."

"Husband," she called over to him, "build up the fire for our guest while I put the kettle on and fry some bread."

For one so complacent only a moment before, the old man's wife bustled around their one room cabin setting their simple table for toast and tea.

The stranger's eyes followed her every move. A large man, with a full beard that cascaded down the front of his shirt, he pulled out a leather purse from his wide belt. His large fingers clumsily opened it up and he drew out two large golden coins.

"Here," he said, placing them gently onto the table. "This will cover my meal and bed for the night. I will have more for you in the morning."

The old woman greedily swiped the coins into her hands and hid them into the folds of her apron.

After their humble meal, the visitor sat in the Morris chair next to the fire and pulled out a pipe. While he puffed away, enjoying the cheerful fire, the old woman whispered into her husband's ear, "You must give him our bed and cover him with our heavy quilt. We will sleep on a blanket on the floor. We must be sure that he sleeps soundly."

Her exasperated husband brought the stranger to the far side of the cabin to the bed that only he and his wife shared since the night of their marriage 45 years ago.

By the time the old man returned to the table, where his wife sat mesmerized by the golden gleam of the two coins basking in the lamplight, the stranger was already snoring loudly in a deep sleep.

In the dwindling light of the fire, the old man and his wife spoke in soft tones at the table.

"He seems like a very strong man," he said. "Perhaps the first stroke would not be enough," he surmised.

"It will be easy," she said, mesmerized by the glimmering coins she held in her hand. "See how he sleeps upon his back. I will stand beside you with the ax."

"He's a large man, and there will be much blood," he cautioned her.

"Not to worry, husband," she said calmly. "There is a storm outside our door. We can bury him in the snow, and by tomorrow morning, the wolves will have had their fill of him. If anyone comes looking for him, we can say that he arose early and left—or that he never even came here at all! He has a purse full of gold, I saw it glimmering in the light of our fire when he drew out the coins!"

"I don't have the heart to murder a man in his sleep," he protested. "See how my hands tremble, so."

"You are a fool, husband!" his wife snarled. "Here," she said, thrusting one of the two gold coins into his hands. "Go to the pub and drink up enough courage to come back and do what is needed to help us survive this winter. If you are not back in an hour, I will slit his throat myself!"

He took the coin without a response and opened the door to the blizzard raging outside.

"All men are cowards and fools," his wife muttered to herself, locking the large door behind him.

At the pub, where the men from the village gathered for warmth, a few laughs and most importantly, time away from their nagging wives, the old man drank one pint after another, and with plenty of money left over, he was in a good mood to help his friends forget all about their own troubles by buying them round after round of ale.

Losing the track of time, the hours passed into the wee hours of the morning with great joviality.

As the inn keeper was about to close the pub, he poured the old man one last pint, wondering where his sudden wealth came from.

"Do you drink to forget, my friend, or do you drink for joy because your son has returned?"

The old man put his pint glass down on the bar and grimaced at the inn keeper with a look of horror in his eyes. "What do you mean, my son?"

"Yes, he came here earlier and was asking around if you and your wife still lived in a one room cabin up on the hill. He told us that he was planning a big surprise for his mother and father. I didn't know him at first, since he has since gained a lot of weight and has grown a great beard, but after a few minutes, I recognized him as your estranged son, Wesley."

Combustible

Nothing much ever happens in the New England town of Dunstable, New Hampshire. In its heyday during the 1920's, it was one of the richest exporters of high-quality granite, known for unique colors and marbling that would be difficult, if not impossible, to find anywhere else in the world. After the Wall Street crash in 1929, the town stopped growing, and when the once-rich veins and quarries of granite were exhausted, that was when the people of Dunstable began to leave for good.

There isn't anything today that would attract folks to Dunstable with its population of 444. It is one of those small country towns that you would miss if you blinked while driving through it, but for the people who make it their home, they like the pastural scenery, the four seasons and the intimacy of a small community. It is one of those proverbial, 'tight-knit' towns that have a kind of intimacy you don't get to experience in the big city. Everyone knows each other by name, and this can be a good thing, but it can also be a disadvantage, and in some cases, downright nasty.

It was a Saturday morning, not unlike any other morning, when the picturesque country stores and shops along both sides of Main Street opened for business at exactly 8:00.

Keslinger's General Store had been a barn before Henry Keslinger converted it into a convenience store with a small deli. Two years ago, he sold his huge farmhouse across the street to make room for an Exxon gas station, now the only gas station in town, complete with a full auto service section and hydraulic lift. The modern-styled gas station was located on the corner of Main Street and Merrimack Road, where the library occupied the opposite corner. Behind the library, further up Merrimack Road stood the 1st Congregation Church of Dunstable, with the parsonage next to it, and where Rev. Eustice Wright lived with his pretty wife, ready to give birth to their firstborn any day now. A stone's throw from the parsonage was the police station, recently converted from the town's original one-room schoolhouse. The new school, another mile or so further up the road, was named after Dunstable's first school founder and principal, Crispin M. Peabody.

The Gilmour family lived on Elementary Lane. Fred Gilmour was the current principal of the new school. He owned a restored 1973 Volkswagen Super Beetle, but he didn't need to use it, except in bad weather, since it was only a five-minute walk to the school. His wife, Muriel, never learned to drive a standard, so she had her own car, a used, '74 Dodge Dart Swinger automatic, which everyone in town recognized because of its hideous lime-green color.

Across the street from the Gilmour's, lived Alexander "Lex" MacBride and his wife, Linda—together with their 17-year-old daughter, Janet. Lex owned his own car and truck repair shop. He once had a gas pump too, but he could not keep up with the new Exxon station, so he ended up serving as the local mechanic for folks on a fixed income: repairing lawn mowers, motorcycles, snowmobiles, and farming equipment. Business is not what it used to be since he also lost his tire and inspection services to the better pricing that Exxon offered. Exxon even tried—on more than one occasion—to hire Lex as their lead mechanic, but he couldn't bear not being his own boss, especially after 30 years as the only gas station and repair station in town. Everybody knew him as the kind of guy that would bend over backwards to make his customers happy and then he would allow them to pay their bill as much as they could when they could without keeping tabs.

The Gilmour's had a 15-year-old son, Oliver, but, as you can already imagine, everyone called him 'Ollie' (though he was also known in school, much to his chagrin—and with no thanks to his father's vocation—as "Oily"). His mother was nine months pregnant, ready to deliver any day now, and he was really hoping for a baby sister, which he thought would make his mother very happy.

He had a paper route. He and his golden retriever, Boatswain, were a common sight every day when he delivered newspapers on his black 3-speed Apollo Stingray bicycle with his dog by his side. He had a crush on his neighbor Janet, but the difference between 15 and 17 is like 10 years in teenage time. He was completely head-over-heels in love with her, but she barely noticed him. He was just a sophomore, and she was a senior. One more year, and she would be off to college, kicking the dirt of this town from her shoes forever.

On this particular Saturday, it seemed like half the town was crawling all over main street like ants doing their grocery shopping at Bickford's, getting haircuts, browsing Woolworth's, the local five and dime, the Paperback Booksmith—and getting breakfast at one of the three restaurants in town.

JoAnn's Diner was the most popular. It was an actual diner car from an old train company that she and her husband, "Moose" LeBlanc, fixed up with cheap paneling, frilly curtains and red vinyl reupholstered booth benches and barstools. JoAnne used her huge collection of '50's and '60's 45 RPM records as her motif. Wherever you sat in the diner, you were surrounded by these old 45's hanging on the walls: "Runaround Sue" by Dion; "My Boyfriend's Back" by The Angels; "Happy Together" by The Turtles; "Somebody to Love" by the Jefferson Airplane, and so on. Since almost everyone in town smoked, the once-white hanging ceiling was now a dingy yellow, but aside from the chintzy decor, the plentiful servings of food and coffee was great and the prices even better. It was always full to capacity up until lunchtime when they closed, and then JoAnn and Moose spent the rest of the day fishing in Horseshoe Pond or in the streams of Twin Bridges. In the summer's, depending on the weather, they would take their boat to Massachusetts for some deep-sea fishing too.

It was just another typical Saturday morning. Henry Keslinger leaned against his broom outside his store talking to Archie O'Connor, the owner of 'O'Connor's New and Used Cars' next door. A small gang of teenagers were throwing chestnuts at each other from the two chestnut trees that provided shade on the front lawn of the library.

"Knock it off, you kids!" Henry shouted from across the street.

One of the kids gave him the finger and another kid mooned him before they all ran away with mocking laughter.

"I know your parents, you crazy kids! I know where you live!" Archie shouted through a near toothless mouth, raising a beer can in his hand, his second one since he got out of bed.

Main street was busy on this particular Saturday morning. The weather was cooler than average for September, which is why so many folks were out and about running errands and stopping to catch up on the latest news and gossip. It was a near perfect morning.

Suddenly an ear-piercing scream cut through everyone's chatter. Folks looked around at each other wondering where it came from, but more than this, for what reason?

A person—it was difficult to tell whether it was a man or a woman, a boy, or a girl—was running down Merrimack Road to the intersection with Main Street. The unknown person was completely engulfed in flames.

"Help me!" the poor creature screamed. "Make it stop! Put it out!"

People separated, making a path for the human ball of fire, not knowing what to do. Finally, a man jumped out of the crowd and pushed it down onto the street right in front of the general store and tried to use his jacket to put out the flames, but it was instantly consumed by the fire, and then he fell back himself with both of his hands covered in 3rd degree burns. Others threw their own autumn jackets over the blazing fire, but the incredible heat instantly consumed these as well.

Henry dropped his broom and ran into his store, emerging seconds later with a fire extinguisher, but this only seemed to make the fire bigger, brighter, and hotter. No one knew what to do, so in bewildered frustration, they all stood in a circle, four people thick, and watched the intensity of the strange fire slowly decrease until there was nothing left of this unknown person in the middle of Main Street. No body, no skeleton . . . nothing but a large, black scorched spot where a living human body had been just a moment before.

No one said a word for what seemed like a long time.

"Lord God, almighty," Archie said, slurping a sip from his beer can, "Did you see that?"

Three or four men were attending to the man's burned hands, and lifting him up, brought him to the library until an ambulance from nearby Johnson City would come pick him up.

"Where's Phil and Ted?" someone said in a daze. "Anyone gone to get Phil and Ted?"

Phil Labrie and Ted Harkins were the entire police force for Dunstable. Sure enough, someone ran up the hill behind the library to the police department and brought them down to the scene in their single patrol car with sirens blaring and with as many piercing red and blue lights flashing as they could turn on. After all, this was the biggest deal since the gruesome suicide of old man Reed two years ago when he somehow managed to saw himself in two using his own sawmill.

"Move out of the way," Officer Labrie shouted, as he roughly moved his way through the crowd. "C'mon now, get outta the way—let me in! Let me see what's going on, for cryin' out loud, move out of the way!"

When Phil reached the black spot in the road, he looked over to Henry and Archie and said, "What—this is it?"

"You don't understand," Archie belched, pointing to the sooty spot, "This was a person!" The crowd supported him with groans of acknowledgement.

"So, where's the body?" Phil asked, asking the obvious.

"That's the thing," someone said. "There *was* a body. Someone was screaming their lungs out, running down the street—you shoulda seen 'im—with their arms in the air, shoutin' and hollerin' for help, but we couldn't do nuthin'. We tried, but anything we did didn't do nuthin'. Even when Henry was trying to douse it with his fire extinguisher, it was like pouring gasoline onto the fire."

By this time, officer Harkins reached the center of the circle. "What do you want me to do, Chief?" he asked.

Phil shook his head and removed his cap. "Do? There's nothing here but a cock and bull story, Ted."

Phil instructed the crowd to disperse and instructed Henry to place some orange cones that he used for his snow-plowing side-business around the scorched area on the street. "I also want a tarp over it until I can figure out what's going on," Phil instructed.

Wiping his balding head with a handkerchief before putting his cap back on, Phil repeated his order for everyone to get off the street and go about their business.

"Ted, you stay here and make sure no one comes near this. Get yourself a coffee from Henry and then keep an eye on it from the patrol car. I'm going to get some statements from folks that witnessed this thing, or whatever it was."

Around this time, Ollie was coasting down Merrimack Road on his Stingray to pick up his papers from Keslinger's for his paper route.

"Hey, what's going on, Mr. Keslinger?" Ollie asked, sticking a piece of Bazooka bubble gum into his mouth.

"We had an incident," Henry replied. "The police are looking into it. Best that you just collect your papers and get going."

COMBUSTIBLE

Ollie shrugged his shoulders and loaded his large orange canvas newspaper sack with the papers and pushed his bike up the steep Merrimack Road until he got to the parsonage, his first stop.

About 100 feet from the parsonage, Boatswain stopped and would not go any further.

"What gives, boy"? Ollie smiled, turning his head back to his faithful companion. Then the slight odor of something putrid, like rotten eggs, crept into his nose. However, as soon as he noticed it, it was gone, and so was Boatswain's strange behavior.

Rev. Wright was sitting on his porch overlooking Main Street, smoking a cigar, and drinking a beer. Ollie thought it was odd for a minister to be drinking in the morning, not to mention the cigar, but he minded his own business and walked up to the porch with the pastor's paper.

"Hi, Pastor Wright," Ollie said cheerfully, with the paper tucked under his arm. Today was collection day.

"Good morning, Oliver," the pastor responded. "Here are your dues, along with your tip," holding out two small envelopes in his hand.

"Thank you, Pastor," Ollie said, taking them, "and here's your paper."

"Thanks," the minister said, in a cloud of smoke.

"Did you hear about the incident in front of the library?" Ollie asked.

"Yes, I heard some commotion, but I'm meditating, son."

"Yes Sir, of course . . . I'm sorry I interrupted you, Pastor. Well, have a nice day. We'll see you in church tomorrow."

As Ollie walked back to his bike, opening the tip envelope, he growled to himself, "Dumb! Stupid! Idiot! Interrupting a man of God during prayer, like that . . . " He opened the envelope wider, dissatisfied with the pastor's tip and hoping to find more. "Nice," he muttered sarcastically, "50 lousy cents. He's the worst tipper on my route."

Two hours later, Ollie completed his route, and as he rode his bike into his driveway, Boatswain made a dash for the MacBride's house across the street, where Janet was sitting on her lawn, reading a magazine.

"Drats!" Ollie said under his breath. "Now I gotta go over there and get that dumb mutt of mine. She's just gonna think I'm looking for an excuse to bug her."

He walked across the street and tried to act nonchalant. Boatswain was slobbering her chin and neck with his big, fat tongue, and she seemed to be OK with it, but what would he say once he got his dog under control? He knew she could care less about him. She was two years older, and he heard around school that she was keen on Doug Thompson, the senior with the perfect teeth, the square jaw, blonde hair, wall-to-wall muscles and already bragging to everyone about going to Harvard next fall.

"Hey, what's up?" she said smiling into the sun, rubbing Boatswain's neck.

"Not much. I just finished my paper route. Sorry he's bothering you."

"It's no bother, Ollie, I love this mutt! He can bother me anytime. By the way, did you hear about the craziness down by the gas station this morning?"

"All I know is that there was some sort of explosion on Main Street between the library and Exxon and someone got burned."

"Yeah, right, someone on fire and running amuck. They had to send out for an ambulance from Johnson City for a man who got injured when he tried to put out the flames. No one's saying much else."

"What happened? The gas station is right there on the corner. Was it some sort of accident—perhaps something to do with the new gas pumps?"

"I don't know. Someone was on fire, but no one knows who it was. More than this, there is no body—no remains whatsoever—not even a ring or a watch. The body and everything associated with it was completely consumed."

"C'mon, what d'ya mean, '*no remains*'?"

"That's just it—no one can figure out who it was."

"Well, it should be pretty easy to figure out since there are now only 443 people remaining in this town."

"That's a really good point, Ollie."

At 79 years old, Jesse Metcalf was the oldest resident in Dunstable, yet he continued to live alone in his cottage by Horseshoe Pond, miles away from the smalltime hustle and bustle of Main Street. He remembered the good times when the town was growing rapidly during the 1920's. He was the town's Sheriff back in those days until he retired 10 years ago, when the town was reduced to being more like a quaint photo on some New England postcard that you would likely find in a dusty rack in gas stations and convenience stores across the state.

There was little crime back in those days. The worst case he ever dealt with regarded an old woman who thought she was a witch. Her name was Garnet Fuld, and she was accused of placing a curse on Dunstable when it fell under exceedingly difficult times, especially during the years of the great Depression. A dozen children went missing between 1930 and 1933, and she was accused of their demise. The town's Chamber of Commerce at that time tried to get her to leave the town, but she would not budge.

As he did from time to time with the older folks in town, Sherriff Metcalf paid her a visit one day in early October 1934, and found her shack burned to the ground. Her body was never recovered. He tried to investigate the matter further, but the case went cold, and to this day, most of the older folks still believe the town's inability to grow is in part to what happened to the old woman, or more to the point—the curse she ostensibly placed over it.

Born in 1900, Jesse had been in two world wars and had seen everything from prohibition to the birth of rock and roll to the civil rights movement, the deaths of the Kennedy boys and Watergate. Since retirement, he took one trip to New York City to visit his sister—even got the chance to tour the Statue of Liberty—and then a short vacation in Yellowstone National Park, but aside from his military campaigns overseas and these trips, he lived his entire life in Dunstable.

All of his friends are dead, not a single one left. His wife, Daisy, died from lung cancer in '67 and he's been alone ever since. He minds his own business and expects others to do the same, except for his young friend, Ollie Gilmour, who rides his bike to his cabin on the pond each Saturday afternoon with leftover newspapers from the prior week. Jesse never throws anything away—a real pack rat he is. In the winter, he pads his legs and arms with old newspapers under his clothes to keep himself warm. There is so much rubble in his cabin, that it is a fire waiting to happen, especially with his pipe-smoking and an old wood stove in need of repair.

Ollie loaded up the past week's newspapers, a few magazines that his father no longer read, and four cans of SpaghettiOs that he nicked from his mother's pantry. Jesse loved SpaghettiOs. He jumped on his bike, and with Boatswain trotting beside him, he peddled the four miles to Jesse's cabin.

When he arrived at the old man's place, he leaned his bike up against a huge pine tree in front of the cabin, slung the sack over his shoulder, and walked to the front door where he rapped on it with the friendly code that was reserved just for friends: 'Knock, knock—knock-KNOCK-knock.'

"C'mon in boy!" Jesse said with a raspy cough. "The door's unlocked, just c'mon right in."

Ollie opened the screen door and let it slam behind him. "I brought your papers, Mr. Metcalf, and I also brought a couple National Geographic's and Time magazines that my dad was gonna throw away."

"That's my boy," Jesse said, slowly working himself out of his recliner.

"And look what else I have for you," Ollie said, reaching dramatically into his canvas newspaper sack, "Four cans of your favorite!"

"Good show!" Jesse exclaimed sliding his hands together. "Thank you so much! What do I owe you?"

"Nothing, Mr. Metcalf, it's my pleasure."

"Aw, c'mon now, lad, I know you took these from your Mama's cupboard. Let me at least pay you for these."

"No Sir!" Ollie retorted. My mother's never gonna miss 'em, since I'm the only one that will eat this crap." They both laughed.

"I know what you mean," Jesse said, slipping his dentures into his mouth. "But with a lot of pepper and some shake cheese, it ain't so bad."

After Ollie put the cans of SpaghettiOs away, he went back to the front door to let Boatswain in. Boatswain immediately gravitated toward Jesse, who had slunk back down into his cozy green leather recliner, and then covered the dog with long strokes along his back.

"Mr. Metcalf," Ollie said somberly. "There was an incident in town this morning."

"Yeah? Like what?" Jesse enquired, thumbing through a magazine.

"Someone was running around on fire. A man nearby tried to douse the flames, but he only ended up getting hurt in the process. Whoever it was that was on fire... he, or she, burned up so bad.... and there wasn't anything left. Nothing, nothing at all. I wasn't there to see it, but this is what I heard."

Jesse stopped patting the dog and seemed to look through Ollie's eyes, which were still transfixed on the old man's glassy glare, as though waiting for a response. He awkwardly maneuvered himself out of the recliner again and walked past Ollie over to the window above his sink. He placed both hands on the warped, pine countertop. The expression on his face slowly turned from one of shock into sheer rage. "Damn!"

"Mr. Metcalf?" Ollie asked, probingly.

"You say, no one seems to know who it was?"

"I'm not sure, but from what I know, there's no way to identify who it was. This person was engulfed in flames, and the screams could have been from a man or a woman—no one knows. There is nothing left but a black, sooty spot in the center of Main Street. It's still there covered by a tarp, which I saw when I went to collect the papers for my route. I was thinking that, since we know the population of the town, the missing person should be easy enough to figure out."

"Good thinking, Ollie, but I want you to do exactly as I say, ya hear me boy?"

"Yes Sir, of course . . . "

"I'm going to give Labrie a call, but for now, I want you to go home and stay there. On your way home, I want you to ride as fast as you can. You need to get there before it gets dark in about an hour. Promise you will do exactly as I say."

"Yes, Mr. Metcalf," Ollie responded, dutifully, "I will do just as you say, but can I still come over after Church tomorrow?"

"Yes, of course—you do that. Now git!"

Along the bike ride back home, with Boatswain trailing behind him, Ollie shifted his Apollo Stingray into third gear and began thinking that perhaps, Mr. Metcalf was starting to become a bit senile. He was, after all, an old man, and what was all this business about getting home before dark? Regardless, he was actually a little relieved to pull into his driveway just before the sun dipped below the tall trees in the distance. He went to bed after watching some television, looking forward to seeing Jesse the next day.

First thing after he and his parents returned home from Church, Ollie got on his bike, and with Boatswain beside him, he peddled as fast as he could through the shortcut in the woods to get to Jesse's cottage. When He got there, the entire place was burned to the ground. He got off his bike and let it fall like a rock to the scorched earth. Boatswain backed away with his tail between his legs and whimpered restlessly.

Ollie walked through the rubble and could not believe his eyes. Everything was gone. He could not locate a single item that manifested its original form. It was as though the entire cottage was blown up, and then incinerated ten times over.

While Ollie kicked away at the smoldering debris, he heard a siren in the distance. It got louder and louder until it shut off with the arrival of the town's lone police car.

"What're you doing here, Oliver?" Phil asked, impatiently.

"I just came by to visit Mr. Metcalf. We made plans yesterday."

"You saw him yesterday?" he inquired.

"Yes Sir."

"The poor old man must have fallen asleep smoking in bed," Phil surmised.

Ollie kept silent. He knew that Jesse loved his pipe but was not remiss enough to permit such a mishap, especially with hoarding so much junk in his home.

"I'm going now," Ollie said, picking up his bike.

"Yeah," Phil said, shaking his head at the wreckage. "You do that, and don't make a big thing out of this—there's a perfectly good explanation and it has nothing to do with what happened yesterday."

It was 11:00 at night and with his parents asleep in bed, he took the chance to slip out of his house to cross the street and fling a few pebbles at Janet's bedroom window.

She opened the window, and blinking away the sleep from her eyes, she looked down and saw Ollie standing there.

"What do you want?" she asked with a yawn.

"Mr. Metcalf is dead," he said, "his entire place was completely burned beyond recognition, just like the person from yesterday. Can you come down? We gotta talk!"

"Give me a minute, I'll be right down."

On the front lawn, where she had been the day before reading magazines, Ollie waited for her. He paced back and forth nervously. "Dumb! Stupid! Idiot!" he said, slapping his head. "She's gonna think I'm such a fool."

She came out into the moonlight in a thin robe. Ollie was captivated by her loveliness, but his fear overrode the raging of his teenage hormones.

"Listen, something really weird is going on here. I was at old man Metcalf's cottage this morning and it was leveled—I mean, totally leveled from fire—just like that—whoever it was—person from Saturday."

"And what about Mr. Metcalf—you say he's dead?"

"Totally! But yesterday, when I was telling him what happened on the street between the library and Keslinger's, his whole demeanor changed. He was completely overwhelmed with anger, and then he made me promise to get back home before dark, like something straight out of a 'Twilight Zone' episode."

"OK—I'm not actually following . . . "

"Don't you get it?" Ollie interrupted. "There's a connection here. The dead person in the street; some old hag's curse over the town; Mr. Metcalf's knowing something more about all of this and then going through the same ordeal himself. It's like something or someone is trying to erase people from this town, leaving nothing behind. If Mr. Metcalf was erased for something he may have known about, then perhaps that person in the street was erased for having found out something they shouldn't have. Don't you get it? Now both you and I know something about—who knows, what—but maybe this is enough to get us erased too!"

In a bright flash, Ollie and Janet suddenly found themselves surrounded by five men in black hooded cloaks, instantly recognizable to them: police officers Phil Labrie and Ted Harkins, Henry Keslinger, Archie O'Connor, and Pastor Wright.

"What's this?" Ollie asked excitedly. "Where'd you come from!" Janet came close and wrapped her arms around him, shivering from the evening chill, but perhaps more from the fear of these men dressed in black.

"You two think you're so smart, don't you?" Pastor Wright said. "You think that this town can survive without that witch's curse? "444 . . . no more, no less—invert the '444' and you get a '666!" We continue to be a town because we have no choice but to abide by her curse. No more, no less; the survival of this town depends on it!

"That woman we incinerated yesterday insisted on moving into our town of 444."

"*No more, no less,*" the others chanted.

"She was one of those so-called, 'New York artists,' who planned to set up a boutique and a fancy gallery in our beloved town, which would have only brought in more people from the city, more unbelievers!

"*No more, no less,*" the others chanted.

We tried to persuade her to leave, but she wouldn't, so we invoked the curse, and by doing so, we preserved our population of 444 to maintain the equilibrium of our town."

"That doesn't make any sense!" Ollie interrupted. If you are also responsible for Mr. Metcalf's death, then you are down by one, and if you do away with the two of us, then you're down by three!"

The coven laughed, mockingly.

"Don't you get it, paper boy?" Henry chuckled, "The Wright's just had twins and your own mother just gave birth to a baby girl!"

Matthew

For a 12-year-old boy, it was hard to believe that Matthew never played games with family or friends. No checkers or card games—like Old Maid, Solitaire or War—and certainly, no board games like the ones all of his friends seemed to have: Monopoly, Life, Battleship, and Risk . . . All he had to play with were his G.I. Joe's and an assortment of little green, plastic Army figures. Matthew was never bored with keeping his own company and entertaining himself for hours in his imaginary world, except when his mother would interrupt, like she did tonight.

"Matthew!" his mother shouted from the kitchen, like she usually did, "put your toys away and take out the garbage, I'm sick of looking at it!"

But this night, she went too far.

"Okay, guys," he said to his toy soldiers as he carefully held them in his hands, "she's going to make us go out into the darkness again. Just be ready, okay?"

I still do not know if it was just Matthew, or if all kids his age know about "things in the dark," but he knew "things" were out there, only his mother never believed him.

"Matthew!" his mother shouted again, only this time with a notable hint of irritation, "The garbage!"

"Coming, Mom, sheesh!"

"What did you say?"

As Matthew walked into the kitchen, he knew he was wrong with the disrespectful tone he used in responding to his mother, but he also knew too well that there were those "things" out there, but she would never listen to him, always assuming his imagination was getting the better of him.

"I was just putting away my soldiers, except for Captain Jack and Sgt. Pendleton," he said, pulling them out of his pocket.

"Just once, can't you do without them? After all, they are just toys . . . You can't carry these around with you day and night forever! Leave them on the kitchen counter and take out the garbage; I'm not going to ask you again."

"OK, Mom," he said with a shrug.

Matthew grabbed a handle of the kitchen garbage can and using his elbow, he flipped open the kitchen screen door latch. He thought, 'My soldiers are my best friends. I cannot believe my own mother is sending me out into this dark, dank alley to empty this god-forsaking garbage! I cannot begin to count the number of times when my soldiers pulled me back from the slobbering jaws of hideous death. "Toy" soldiers, she calls them, and now, here I am in this alley without them to protect me! "Please God, don't let anything happen to me!"

His heart sank when he saw that the dumpster was all the way down at the end of the alley, but in the dimly lit backstreet, it probably seemed further away than it actually was. Yet, the huge, green container sat there like an oversized coffin for garbage, rubbish, and filth. He read in *True Crime* magazine recently that a murderer used such a dumpster to hide the body of a dismembered woman he had killed. A homeless man collecting empty soda and beer cans found her in a garbage bag a few days later.

As he tugged and pulled the over-sized kitchen waste can down the alley, he wondered why his mother never asked him to take on such a task during *the daytime*. He would have been more than willing—delighted, even—to empty the trash during *the daytime*, when all sorts of "things" do not lurk around in the darkness and the shadows—just waiting for someone, like himself, to stumble by with a loaded garbage can full of the leftovers and expired food that only they could appreciate.

Suddenly, he heard a movement to his left. It sounded slithery and wet. Then there was a similar noise to his right, and just behind him he heard a sort of fluttering sound like giant bat wings. His heart began beating so hard and fast, that he was sure that the "things" could hear it. He stopped pulling the kitchen garbage can and stood silently hoping that by doing so, the "things" would not hear him and perhaps, forget all about him and move on.

Suddenly, a diabolic shriek shattered his thoughts, and peering over his shoulder, he saw one of those "things" rise out of a long shadow among the metal trashcans lining the alley wall. It towered above him with a menacing snarl, its winged claws outstretched and its fangs dripping with gummy drool.

"Help! Momma! It's got me! It's got me!"

She never came to his rescue.

However, all was not yet lost, for had it not been for his honed reflexes and lighting fast reactions, Matthew would never have made it back to the kitchen door before that monster caught him in its clutches. It was a near miss. This was too close, much to close to chance again. If only he had his soldiers with him . . .

Yet, Matthew soon found himself running from one horrible scene into another, for as soon as he burst in through the screened kitchen door without the garbage can, his mother beat him mercilessly with a belt, shouting, "I promised your father that the next time you started screaming about monsters in the dark, that I'd beat your bottom. Believe me, this is for your own good!"

"Well, she's really done it this time," Matthew thought, crying into his pillow. He was beginning to feel about her the same way that he felt about those "dark things" out there. He was never certain what to believe about his toy soldiers, or where they really came from. His mother said that she bought them for him one Christmas from an old German neighbor in the apartment building who needed money; ostensibly a former Nazi. Out of curiosity, Matthew researched the ideology of the Nazi's at the library when he was supposed to be working on a lame social studies report. He learned that the German soldiers were forced to take methamphetamines to keep from sleeping during the few days it took them to reach, and then successfully conquer Poland, and that Hitler used the occult to help him in his strategies to conquer the world.

While he hugged his pillow close to his face, wiping the tears from his eyes, he looked over to the toy soldiers lined up in rows on his dresser, curiously illuminated by the moonlight bleeding in through the blinds of his bedroom window.

The olive drab green plastic soldiers were remarkably interesting. Some lay low in the prone position holding a rifle. Others were kneeling on one knee pointing a machine gun, and there were many more in various positions and using a variety of weapons. These were the toy soldiers his mother got from the Nazi.

"Matthew!" his mother shouted, fragmenting his reminiscence of the best Christmas, ever. "You get yourself right back outside and bring the garbage can back in! Get out of bed and go get it, right now!"

"She's got to be kidding me," he lamented, wagging his head, while slipping his cold feet into his sneakers.

As he wiped his face of tears and blew his leaking nose into his sheet, he looked at his toy soldiers meticulously lined up on his dresser, as though they were looking at him, waiting for an order.

He suddenly recalled the day when the bully, Fat Frank worked him over wicked bad. For many nights lying on his bed, how he wished those "things" would suddenly appear and take out his revenge on Fat Frank. Matthew then recalled how his toy soldiers had mysteriously glowed for the first time one night. The next morning, the newspapers and televised news reporters claimed that 14-year-old, Francis Ramone, was found in an alley in pieces, as though a pack of wild dogs had torn him limb from limb, and this is based on what they found *remaining* of him . . .

"Matthew! The garbage!" his mother shouted.

"Mom—just a minute, I'll be right there!"

"That's it! Just wait until your father gets home! I'll get the garbage can myself!"

"No, Mom! I'll go . . . I'm just putting on my sneakers! I'll show you that I am not afraid of the dark!"

"For the last time, Matthew, nothing is out there!" his mother yelled from the kitchen.

"But don't go out there now, mother—not *now!*"

Little did she know, but through her son's tears, he had asked his soldiers to send out a specialized task force to kill all intruders, no matter who or what they are. He wanted them *dead*. All he could do now was to lock the kitchen door and pray that he would remain safe during the horrible encounter his mother was doomed to. He felt a little sad when he caught himself fighting away a grin that was struggling to emerge on his face.

As Matthew sat huddled in the fetal position up against the kitchen door, he began to hear movements: gross, slithering, wet sounds that he was familiar with so many nights before in the alley when having to face the enemy on his own. Then he heard his mother scream. It was a surprised sort of scream at first, like when a friend comes up behind you and spooks you in a practical joke kind of way, but then the real screaming began. The gurgling screams were the most unpleasant for

Matthew to bear, such that he had to plug his ears with his fingers and grit his teeth until the screaming finally stopped.

The insidious grin he successful fought off moments before suddenly returned as it made its crooked path across his thin lips when he considered just how little pity his mother had for him when he found himself in her current position. It was difficult keeping the kitchen door locked, but she deserved it. He knew what his mother was going through, but all he wanted was for her to finally acknowledge his own experiences—what he had been going through himself all this time.

Dad got home about an hour later. Matthew was not worried though.

Everything had ended just fine.

Mother had seen his point. She finally came to understand that he was not being silly or childish or immature about the "dark things." It was all going to be different now. Matthew's father acknowledged this himself when he saw his wife in pieces on the kitchen floor with all of Matthew's toy soldiers surrounding her and with a kitchen knife sticking out of her neck.

Now all Matthew needed to do was to take Dad out into the alley to show him the dark things like he showed his mother, and with just a little imagination, all would be well for Matthew.

Hagberry Pot

"Alex!" his twin brother, Charles, screamed out in pain, rubbing his knee. "Why can't you be more careful!"

The twins were running through the orchard of old man Hayward, stealing apples again.

"What is it, little brother?" Alex asked, bending over him, taking a bite out of a large red apple with the juice running down his chin. Charles laid in the shade of one of the apple trees, writhing in agony on the grassy path, rubbing his knee with his hands.

"When you are reckless, I am the one who suffers for the both of us, remember?" he replied, hiding his tears. "I feel the hurt from all of your careless accidents."

"I do too, little brother," Alex shrugged, "but it's not a big deal. C'mon," he said, snatching another bite, "we gotta get moving before old man Hayward catches up with us."

"You just need to be more careful," Charles said, standing up.

"Alright!" Alex snapped, "but let's get out of here. Remember the last time when the old geezer shot at us with rock salt?"

Alex led the way, with his brother limping behind him up over the hill. Down the hill beneath a grove of towering trees, they lived with their mother and father in Gight Castle. Their father, Sir George Byron, was the Laird of over 2500 acres. Near the castle lay Hagberry Pot, a bottomless water hole with legends and mysteries all of its own.

"Do you think old man Hayward saw us?" Charles quizzed his brother, panting loudly.

"Don't be ridiculous," Alex responded casually, tossing the apple core away. "If it wasn't for his stupid dog yipping and yapping at us, we could have made off with another dozen apples, no sweat."

"At least we made it this time," Charles said, still nursing his knee, "but I don't want to chance it anymore."

"What?" Alex laughed, mockingly. "You don't want to chance *what* anymore?"

"Getting rock salt shot into my back and legs for one thing, and it's not the nicking of apples, Alex," Charles said angrily, "but I'm tired of taking the pain from your irresponsible behavior and accidents—I get enough scrapes and bruises on my own! I know you do not do it on purpose, but I am not willing to venture any further into these escapades of yours. I want you to leave me out of them for now on."

"Hey, little brother," Alex said, with his flippant attitude suddenly turning sinister. "We're inseparable. I feel what you feel, and you feel what I feel. The only difference is when you cry, moan, and languish in self-pity, I become stronger. Your whining and complaining is so boring! I feel the pain of your clumsiness too, you know, like when you tripped over one of father's croquet wickets on the lawn last week. Did I complain? Yet, when I cause you pain, which is completely unintentional, you just become weaker, which makes me become even stronger. You are, after all, my little brother; I cannot help it if I was born first."

"Yeah, but by only eleven minutes!" Charles barked, standing up. "If I knew that you were only going to drag me to old man Hayward's orchard to steal apples, I never would have gone along with you, but you lied to me. You said it would be a good idea to go exploring like gypsies in search of treasure. Then you fell, while running away from his dogs, and though you felt a degree of pain, it was me who got the brunt of it—look!" Charles raised his swollen knee, covered with bloody lacerations. "Let's see yours!"

Alex lifted the shorts over his knees. They were mildly scraped—not similar in appearance to Charles's deep lacerations.

"We feel each other's pain," Alex said, casually. I cannot help it if I am the elder and you are the runt of the litter.

"Stop saying that!" Charles shouted.

Five years later, when the twins were 18 years old, Lady Grainger and her daughter, Lydia, took rooms at the vacant guest house on the edge of the property of Gight Castle shortly after her husband, Lord Grainger died. He left his wife and daughter with enormous debts in London, and once the money ran out, Lady Grainger showed her birth papers to her Scottish relative, Sir Byron. Since she was also a Byron through the bloodline, he generously offered the guest house to them for as long as they liked.

At 17 years old, Lydia was a beautiful woman, refined in the best that London had to offer young women, and through an unfortunate twist of fate, she now found herself isolated in a derelict guest house overlooking acres of barley, corn, and wheat. Through her bedroom window, she could see cruck houses populated all over the countryside and hundreds of white flecks that made up the sheep grazing in the fields and on the hills. With her father now dead and buried, she lost her position in the powerful circles of the London aristocracy and was now limited to what there was of any in the Formartine area of Aberdeenshire where she now lived with her mother. She understood her options for any future security were exceptionally limited, and the pool of men from which to draw a husband even more so.

Around the same time, there was an incident involving Hagberry Pot. An American came to find the treasures that the Covenanters hid in its depths to avoid confiscation from the English during the Protestant persecution of 1745, when many Scottish castles were destroyed, and when highland kilts and even the bagpipes were forbidden. The American received permission from the Laird to "treasure hunt," as long as 60% of any valuables found went to his estate.

The American, a young, charismatic man associated with the Liberty Foundation of New York, brought along with him two assistants.

The American's name was Eric Browne, an explorer, mountaineer, prospector, and bounty hunter, among other things. He and his men set up a canvas-tent along the serpentine river that emptied into the bottomless pool of Hagberry Pot.

Early their first morning, beneath a sky thick with stormy clouds, one of Browne's assistants got into the water with a rope to tie around the treasures that potentially remained submerged in the depths below. With a deep breath, he dove into the bog, only to have his body resurface moments later in four quarters. The head never surfaced and seemed to have sunk to the depths of the bottomless pool. Browne's second assistant wanted nothing more to do with this excursion until Browne shamelessly held a pistol to his head.

His second assistant dove into the bog only to return to the surface a moment later screaming that he saw the devil himself guarding a magnificent wooden chest reinforced with rusted metal bands. Browne pointed his pistol to the poor man's head and told him that he was not buying it and that he had the choice of getting his brains blown out in the black water of the bog or going back down to tie ropes around the chest so that it could be dragged up to the surface. With no practical choice, the poor man dove back into the black, cold water. Moments later, just like the body of the first man, his body floated to the surface in four quarters—his head also absent among the pieces bobbing in the water.

The American had no choice but to tie a rope around himself and take the dive. He did not believe in monsters or devils, even though the evidence of his hired hands unnerved him. Moments later, he resurfaced with his hands full of gold and precious gems. He tossed them onto the boggy shore and then went back down into the freezing water for more.

Alex was standing on the mossy shore of the bog, looking down at the treasure culled from the cursed pool, laying at his feet. He had no intention of allowing this American to relieve his ancient family of its gold and jewels, so he continued to watch the American retrieve his clan's inheritance, waiting for him to complete the task when Alex would murder him and reclaim 100% of the treasure for himself.

Browne spent the entire day emptying the treasure chest with repeated dives, since he could not free the chest himself. It had become tightly lodged among large, jagged rocks where it was caught on its way to the bottom of the pit, the original tethers having rotted away centuries ago.

Not once did he run into a devil guarding it.

It was becoming dark, and with the daylight giving out, he lifted himself out the pool and stood before Alex like a Greek god, the water on his chest glistening like honey in the light of a fire that Alex built to keep warm while keeping his eye on him. Alex was immediately stuck by his musculature, but more than this, by the gleam of his canines, which protruded from his bluish lips like pearls in the light of the fire.

One afternoon, Lydia took a walk through the expansive fields of barley until she reached the stream that she had spied from the guest house earlier that morning. She walked along the stream until she reached a large bog. Ducks were bathing in the flickering lights of the stream along the way, but when she reached the large pool of water—the Hagberry Pot—she saw that no pond life existed. She stood at the mossy edge of the great pool of black water and noticed that all life ceased to exist. No ducks, no singing crickets, belching frogs, or other sounds familiar with stagnate water.

She knelt over the edge of the pool and could not even see her reflection, so black and deep the water seemed, indicating unknown depths.

"Fascinating, isn't it," a gentle voice came from behind.

She immediately stood up and peered over her shoulder, completely surprised.

Reaching out his hand to her, Charles apologized for startling her. She lifted her skirt to her knees and walked up the embankment to where Charles stood with his hand extended, trying to hide the smile he felt rising on his face.

"My father tells me that you are a distant relative of ours and that you may be using the guest house indefinitely. I was tending to the horses when I saw you walking to the river. What do you think of the property?"

"In all honesty, I miss London, but my mother and I are grateful to have family in Scotland. We had no place to go, and now we have all of this! The castle, our guesthouse . . . and all of this beautiful land . . . it seems to stretch on forever!"

"My name is Charles," he said, taking her hand into his. I have a twin brother, Alex."

"Yes, I know, we met last night."

"You met my brother?"

The next morning, Charles awoke with an odd, foul taste in his mouth. He ran to his mirror, and horrified with his reflection, he saw the brown stains of dried blood on his mouth, cheeks, and chin. He quickly—almost violently—washed his face in unbelief and rinsed his mouth repeatedly until the foul taste was gone. Then he took note of the bloody stains on his shirt and on the sheets of his bed.

He ran to his brother's room for help, but it was locked. Charles banged on the door until his mother appeared at the landing of the stairs.

"What's this all about, son?" she asked.

"I need to speak to Alex, at once!" his twin answered. "Why doesn't he answer?"

"He was out very late last night. Leave him be. I'm sure he needs his rest."

Frustrated, Charles ran back to his room and slammed his door closed. His window was open, but he couldn't imagine why with the weather being so cold. The curtains drifted in and out on the early morning breeze. He turned around and looked again at the sheets of his bed, stained dark brown with dried blood, similar in appearance of the shirt he was wearing. How did all of this blood get onto his bed and clothes, he wondered. How did it get onto his face, and more than this, how did it get into his mouth?

Later in the evening, Charles caught up with his brother and demanded an answer, knowing that they both shared each other's experiences, welcomed or not.

"You are such a short-sighted fool," Alex admonished his brother. "That American was a vampire and he enlightened me to the eternal benefits of everlasting life. Join me, and we can live forever!"

"You're out of your mind, brother, what about Lydia? You will never have her," Charles cried.

"You fool! I already have her—she is already mine—in fact, she is *ours!*"

Charles became insane with anger from the horrifying prospect of losing one so young and beautiful to the darkness of his evil twin brother. He searched the room vigorously and took the sword of his family's crest over the fireplace and thrust it deep into his wicked brother's heart.

He straddled him and plunged the blade into his twin repeatedly until there was nothing but a large gaping hole in his chest. He reached into it, pulled out his shredded heart and flung it into the fire of the hearth, where it seemed to groan in agony as it melted in the flames.

Leaning over his dead brother, Charles intently watched him as he exhaled his last breath on his way to hell.

Exhausted, Charles rolled off of his brother onto his back, and lying beside him, he remembered that he always shared in the experiences of his twin.

Within moments, Charles too was dead.

They Come Back

Charlie Clarke and his three partners in crime were almost finished with their tunnel. In another night or two—three at the most—they planned to elbow and crawl their way through their narrow tunnel beneath the prison wall and out to freedom on the other side. It took them almost a year to complete the job, one painstaking handful at a time, taking turns to dig at the clay-like earth, filling all of their pockets and then emptying them onto the yard the next morning during roll call.

The four of them bunked in a 12x14 cell in the old Catahoula Louisiana prison while the new State prison was under construction seventy miles away. The new prison was going to open in less than two weeks, when Clarke and his men—together with the other 136 inmates—were going to be moved into their new cells with all of the latest technical updates in security. Clarke knew that there would not be any crumbling cell walls to dig through, that's for sure, and no more than two inmates to a cell. He also knew he was cutting it close: they had three days to complete the tunnel, and then that is when they would make their move to freedom.

The summer had been especially miserable with high humidity and an infestation of starving mosquitoes and flies with bellies full of carrion. Since it was nearly impossible to get more than a few hours of sleep each night, digging kept them busy, and being underground in the throat of the tunnel was cooler, with less annoyance from the clouds of annoying insects that the rest of the poor prison inmates had to endure in their miserable, humid cells.

"Blood-sucking bugs," Clarke complained, as he took his turn shimmying into the opening of the tunnel.

At least he would get some relief for an hour or so, forty feet into the tunnel where it was nice and cool, and this was a cake walk, he thought, scooping out bits of clay and stones with a prison spoon that he stole from the dining hall months ago.

"First thing I'm gonna do when I get out of here," he thought, "is get this spoon dipped in gold, and hang it above the stone fireplace of my Alaskan cabin, deep in the wilderness next to a lake." He always wanted to live in Alaska, where he could live in peace and quiet, hunting, trapping, and fishing for his own food and with no one around for a hundred miles in any direction to tell him what he could or could not do. No more police to harass him, no more unbearable heat in the long Louisiana summers, and no blood-sucking bugs! No more people, no diversions, and no temptation! He would truly be free for the first time in his life, and he'd never get into trouble again or have to spend another single day in jail. The mere thought of this made him work even faster. "Three days—max!" he grunted to himself as he dug away at the tunnel.

Then just like he planned, three days later, the tunnel was completed. The four men sat together on a bunk smoking cigarettes and sharing their dreams of their new lives once free. Clarke had come up with the idea of escape a year earlier. The other three men, a brute named Lonny, was given a life sentence for the murder of a gangster from a rival gang in Chicago. Catnap was an oddball given twenty years for embezzlement, and Reggie was in for twelve years for a bank robbery of $250,000 that was never recovered. They never found the cash because Reggie buried it in the town of River Ridge in the deep southern swamps of Louisiana. Reggie was going to make the four of them extraordinarily rich as soon as they escaped from this god-forsaken prison. Yet, at only nineteen years old, Reggie was the physically weakest of the four. In fact, he was the scrawniest man in the entire prison, and he knew his days were numbered until the day he got sent to cell block H, cell 37, which was where he first met Charlie Clarke for the first time. At that time Lonny was already bunking with Clarke and he wanted to have a go at Reggie in a really bad way, but Reggie took Clarke aside and told him about the thousands he had buried in the Louisiana Bayou. From that day on, Reggie was hands-off to any other inmate—especially Lonny. Reggie had become their golden goose. Eventually, even Lonny respected this.

A few weeks later, Catnap got assigned to cell 37. Catnap's real name was Louis Letourneau, and he got his nickname for his unabashed laziness and his reputation of trying to sleep off his incarceration. However, lazy as he was, he knew a good deal when he heard one, and he found a reason to stay awake long enough to participate in the escape for a share in the loot. He didn't have much to offer the others, but he would do his part in the digging, and he'd be quiet about it.

All four men had one thing in common: they wanted to be free, and they wanted to be wealthy. As long as they kept mum about their plan, they would be free men once again, only this time with loads of cash to make life worthwhile for the first time in their lives. They decided it was going to be a 4-way split; Reggie insisted on it.

The big night finally came after a year of planning, dreaming, and slaving away at the tunnel. One by one they each elbowed their way through the narrow passageway until they came out on the other side of the dilapidated prison. On the other side of the fence, they continued to elbow their way into the dense overgrowth of trees and bushes. Once they were away from the dark shadows of the derelict fortress a hundred feet behind them, the lights continued to flood the prison walls as always, but the sirens were deadly silent. They had made it, and they knew it. They were finally free.

They easily commandeered a pickup truck in town and drove the ninety miles to River Ridge to dig up the treasure buried by Reggie before he was apprehended.

When they got there, they spent the next two days searching for the orange ribbons that Reggie had tied to several trees leading to the treasure from a swampy dirt road a mile outside of the insignificant sleepy town.

Losing patience, Lonny threatened to beat Reggie to death if he did not deliver the goods. Lucky for Reggie, Catnap found the first of the orange ribbons that Reggie had tied to the trail of trees leading to the buried treasure. When they arrived at the large willow tree where Reggie buried the $250,000 in a steel box, they each dug excitedly with their bare hands until Lonny's gnarled and bloody fingertips scratched across something hard. It was the steel box that Reggie had stuffed with the stolen money, and now it lay just under an inch of earth!

Like four rats digging for a hidden morsel in the ground, they dug it up and lifted the box onto the mound of earth they made. Opening the box was easy for Lonny—he opened it with his bare hands. Inside the box was everything that Reggie bragged about. Plastic-wrapped blocks of cash, bags of coins and ingots of solid gold.

As they sat back against the heavy darkness of the night, they lit their cigarettes and belched out smoke through smiles of conversation regarding their futures.

Suddenly, a coral snake came out of nowhere and bit Lonny on his thigh. Just as they realized what had happened, Catnip was bitten by another one on his hand. Clarke and Reggie squashed the viper's heads with their heavy prison-issued boots.

"Look around, Reg!" Clarke shouted, as he lifted Lonny up against the trunk of the large willow. "There may be more!" Reggie kicked the debris around the small encampment in search of more snakes, but none were found.

"I think that's all there are," Reggie gasped. "Now what?"

"You need to stay with these two while I try to find help," Clarke said, excitedly. "If I cannot find help, they're goners, so I need to move fast. I saw a light in the distance a quarter of a mile back where we left the truck. I'll go back and see if I can get some help. Keep Lonny and Catnip sitting up against the tree and do not let them fall asleep. I'll be back as soon as I can!"

"Just great!" Clarke said, gnashing his teeth as he raced through the jungle-like terrain, "Just great!" He could not believe how quickly their good luck turned on them. Everything was working out so well! The plan was executed better than he could have ever imagined—all those months digging out of that rat hole—and just as everything was finally coming together, now this!

Finally, he saw a faint yellow light appear through the dense jungle of the swamp. He forged ahead like a man on a mission, not yielding to his chest, which was on fire from exertion and sheer determination. His legs ached and his feet felt like cement blocks. Yet, he made his way closer to the light until—just through an opening in the jungle—he was confronted with an old, run-down mansion from plantation days. Three stories high, with six massive pillars almost completely hidden by ivy and vines, its sheer size caused him to ponder momentarily in sheer amazement.

He bent over with his hands on his knees to catch his breath, never removing his gaze from the antiquated relic of a past age. He focused on a single light illuminating through a window from the third floor. The rest of the house was shrouded in complete darkness, which he thought was strange. "Who would want to live in that wreck of a house all the way out here in the swamp?" he wondered. Yet, time was of the essence. His friends were dying, and there was a fantastic treasure at hand, so he stumbled up to the porch and knocked on the door. A moment later, he heard the clanging of a rusted bolt break free and then the massive front door opened with a terrible creak as though it had not been opened in many years.

A young woman stood before him, holding a candle in her hand. He was completely taken aback to see such a lovely face in the warm, inviting candlelight.

"Can I help you?" she asked with the voice of an angel.

"I'm sorry to bother you," Clarke panted, "but I have some camping buddies about a quarter mile back in the swamp that were bitten by poisonous snakes, and I saw your light in the distance. I wonder if you have clean linen and any medications that might help them."

"Poisonous snakes, oh my," she responded with genuine concern. "We surely have plenty of them. Please come in and let me see what my mother and father can do to help."

When Clarke stepped over the threshold of the massive front door, a gust of wind blew past him with a sickly odor, the kind of scent that rancid meat gives off. He was well acquainted with such a smell from years of eating bad food in the prison dining hall, but this stench was more pronounced. It unnerved him.

In a moment, Clarke watched an elderly couple dressed in old-fashioned clothes make their distinguished presence on the grand staircase. They seemed to come out of nowhere, but since the house was so dark, it really did not register as something out of the ordinary. He was just relieved to interact with people who might be willing and able to help save his partners from their impending doom.

"Our daughter tells us you need help," the old man said, with a distinctive southern accent.

"Yes sir," Clarke replied. "I need a sharp knife, medicine, some whiskey and clean sheets."

As Clarke stood at the base of the great staircase, he soon found himself surrounded by the three strange characters.

"What is your name?" the old gentleman asked, with utterly putrid breath, enough that made Clarke turn his head and cough.

"Charles . . . Charlie Clarke," he nervously replied.

"I knew a Clarke once," the old man chirped up. I purchased most of my slaves from him. He was an honest trader in these parts. So, what brings you here?"

"I have friends, Sir, two friends who were bitten by poisonous snakes. I was hoping that, perhaps, you folks might be able to help me with medicine and clean linens, maybe some spare food and drink? I can pay for it."

"Drink?" the old woman cackled.

"The only drink we are interested in is your blood," the old man laughed.

Suddenly, the three of them were at Clarke's throat, their fangs protruding from thick, red lips.

"Wait!" Clarke screamed. "Hold it!"

The three vampires paused for a moment, perplexed by their victim's defiance.

"You're vampires? For real?"

The three surrounded him, with eyes aflame with desire.

"If you eat me, then that's it, but I have it in my power to offer you three more men, more than enough to keep you well fed for a long time to come. I will lead you to them if you permit me to live, but I must have your word on it. Do vampires know a deal when they see one? Do vampires keep their word?"

The three black figures floated away from the landing where Clarke was left standing, shaking in his boots from sheer terror. Though his mind was racked with disbelief over the situation he was in, he recognized that it was one where he could still come out on top. If these vampires took him up on his offer, they would kill off his three comrades, let him go free and he himself would have access to the treasure all for himself. He proudly smiled from his sudden streak of ingenuity and quick thinking. It could have turned into a hopeless situation, but Clarke knew how to do one thing right, and that was negotiation—even with the devil, if he knew he would benefit from it.

The three demonic creatures returned from their huddle.

"We've discussed it," said the beautiful young woman. "Take us to these men, and you will live, you have our word."

Within moments, Clarke was leading the three vampires to his friends. Along the way, he actually felt a little sorry for what his partners in crime were going to endure. Their throats would be torn to shreds from these fanged monsters, and then the blood of his pals would fill the decrepit bowels of these fiends from hell.

Yet, he'd be spared.

With his three companions out of the way, he would have all of the money to himself! It was a 'win-win' situation as far as he was concerned. So what if these were vampires! He figured he lost more blood to the clouds of mosquitoes over 10 years in prison, only with them, he had nothing to show for it. At least these bloodsuckers were going to give him a paradise on earth, and for the rest of his life.

Once Clarke brought them to the campsite that Catnip made near the huge willow tree, the vampires took no time to devour them. Clarke had to turn away in shame for his betrayal. When they were finished, their bellies bloated with fresh blood, Clarke emerged from the jungle underbrush.

"So, we're square?" Clarke asked, timidly.

With their faces covered in bright red blood, the three vampires stood before Charlie and smiled, their white teeth glistening in the moonlight.

"We're satisfied, you stupid, foolish man, but there is no way that we are going to set you free. Not only can we use this little fortune of yours to our benefit, but we still have need of you."

"You lie!" Clarke screamed, with no impact. "You promised me!"

The three vampires forced Clarke into an old cell in the dank, dark cellar of the mansion, formerly used to punish slaves before the Civil War. Through the next day, as the fiends slept, he looked around in his cell, and could hardly believe that he left one prison cell for another! He laughed to himself from the poetic justice of it all, but being a true escape artist, he spent the day looking for any way of breaking out of the decrepit cage.

In the late afternoon, just before the sun was about to sink beneath the swampy tree line, he found that the door to the cell was mostly corroded, and so he banged away at it with a rock until he was able to break through. He then took large, splintered pieces of a wooden chair and searched for the caskets of the three vampires who betrayed him.

In another room branching off the cellar, he found their caskets.

He opened the first one, and inside it was the old woman with dark, dried blood flaking on the corners of her mouth. "This one's for you,

Grandma!" Clarke shouted with glee as he hammered the large wooden splinter from the chair into her heart and through the bottom of the rotted wood of the casket.

He walked over to the next casket, looked in, and saw the old man looking up at him with eyes pleading for pardon. "This one's got your name on it, old man! Double-cross me, will ya?" Clarke pounded another piece of the broken chair into his chest, destroying him forever.

Finally, Clarke approached the casket of the young woman. He hesitated, admiring her beauty until he focused on her mouth, now blotted with the blood stains from his three friends. "If only I knew you in another time," he whispered, and then he hammered a long-splintered piece of wood into her heart. He stood over her for a moment longer, gazing at her beauty. She was the most gorgeous woman he had ever laid eyes on, but as he fixed his eyes on her angelic face, he watched her face slowly disintegrate into the aged, grotesque old woman that she really was, now free from this curse. Nauseated by the sight, he turned his face away and let the hammer slip out of his slippery, blood-soaked hand to the desecrated earth of the cellar floor.

Now that the dirty business of dispatching these devils was done, he needed to get back out there and pack up his winnings! He whistled a cheerful tune as he made his way back to the willow tree. The last rays of the sun were just beginning to get blotted out by the trees before him as he made his way back to the camp.

"Now with these vampires and my crew dead, I can take it all for myself," he thought, lighting up a cigarette. "I will finally get my lodge in the wilderness of Alaska, with no one to trouble me, ever." He sat down on the mound of dirt next to the tree and considered everything that had just transpired within the last 24 hours. He could hardly believe it—and he knew no one else would, either. "Vampires? Hah!" He lifted the heavy cover of the crate and gorged his eyes on the gold, the huge bundles of $100 bills and large canvas bags of coins. "It's all mine," he thought. "All mine!"

Suddenly, his thoughts of a future filled with spending the stolen lucre on any vice he wanted was interrupted with a snapping twig. Alarmingly, it sounded nearby.

He held his breath. Surely, he had destroyed those three vampires—there was no way they could still be alive. He exhaled quietly and breathed as silently as he could, listening intently... He could hear his own heartbeat pounding with a sense of foreboding.

It was now completely dark, so he lit the lantern that Catnap brought with him the night before.

Pricking up his ears, he nervously took another drag from his cigarette.

Then another snap of twigs in the swamp behind him, and then another. As he doused the cigarette into the soft mound of earth beside him, he held up the lantern only to see Lonny, Catnap and Reggie standing before him.

"You forget," Catnap hissed, "once bitten by a vampire, you become a vampire!"

I will punish them for their ways and repay them for their deeds. They shall eat, but never be satisfied. (Hosea 4: 9-10)

The River

Why do people rush so quickly to their doom? It seems that as soon as they can think for themselves, some scheme and plot nefarious exploits that they believe will make them rich and famous, yet they never read their history!

They hang their hats on the dubious exploits of legends like Billy the Kid, Jesse James, Bonnie and Clyde, Al Capone and so many other notorious, bigger-than life criminals, that they do not take the time to remember their failures, unhappiness, and eventual demise. Each outlaw is guilty of tempting fate, yet they each believe that they are the exception. Such a man was Jimmy the Greek, who lived his life as though he would live forever yet feared death with every breath.

There is still enough cruelty, violence, greed, and lust to haunt a man into dreams of easy money, soft beds, fine food and the best of everything that the world has to offer. However, little thought is spent on just how quickly they hurry to their horrible deaths. Like the old saying goes, "history repeats itself," Jimmy was yet another fool too preoccupied with filling his pockets with easy blood money to ever take note of such historical facts of those losers he idolized.

Jimmy was born into a poor Greek family on the south side of Boston. His father worked two jobs just to put enough food on the table to keep his family from starving during the great depression of the 1930's, and Jimmy's father was one of the lucky ones. After all, he had two jobs, one busing tables in a greasy diner during the day and another job loading delivery trucks with coal in the evenings. Jimmy remembered his old man coming home night after night covered in soot. Then the arguments started . . .

"You aren't making enough money!" his mother shouted. "I'm sick and tired of living in filth!"

One time, as Jimmy slept in his bed, along with four younger brothers and a baby sister, he heard a loud slapping noise from the kitchen downstairs, followed by his mother's crying.

"This is never going to happen to me," Jimmy swore, with tears streaming down his cheeks.

Years later, Jimmy made good on that promise to himself. He had become a soldier for one of the 'Southie' gangs of Boston. Over the years, he climbed the ladder of success in the underworld and became one of the most dependable smugglers in the city. Jimmy knew that they killed a lot of people to get their hands on this particular shipment of gold. He also knew they did other terrible things that he did not like to think about. Yet, they always took good care of him, and he was able to provide a nice home for his mother after his father passed away. His brothers and sister wanted nothing to do with him, but he didn't care. He was living the good life, and he accomplished it all on his own with no help from them.

"Jimmy," one of his gang associates whispered. "This is crazy! We are never going to make it in time. The gold—it's too much—it's too heavy! It's slowing us down, we're gonna get caught!"

"Shut your mouth," Jimmy sneered, "and get this gold to the boat."

"But we're exhausted, Jimmy," grunted another of his crew. "We already have millions in the cargo hold. Let's just drop what we have and get going before it's too late."

"Never!" Jimmy said, running out of patience. "I've worked too hard to lose the largest heist of my career on a bunch of cry-babies. Suck it in and do your job. We've killed too many to get to where we are. There's no going back! Just a few more pallets and then we're out of here!"

"Yeah, but the boat is already too heavy," warned another, "I don't think it can take on any more without sinking, especially if we need to make a run for it. The boat won't hold all of us along with the cargo."

"I don't want to hear any more from you guys. I should have guessed none of you would have the guts to handle a job like this. Any more nagging from you girls and I'll kill you right here and now and keep this fortune all for myself."

One of Jimmy's closest friends came close to him and said, "Jimmy, with all respect, you promised us that this would be an easy job. You said there would be no killing. I will not go to the chair for you, Jimmy. This heist ain't worth it."

"But we're almost finished!" Jimmy argued. "Let's just get this over with. All this worrying and complaining is what's slowing us down!"

The River

Suddenly, a beam of light splintered the dark night from above the hill. It was the police.

"Stop right there!" shouted one of them over a bull horn. "Freeze, or we'll open fire!"

Jimmy laughed to himself. "Go ahead and shoot you idiots. You're too far away to hit me. In another moment I'll have the rest of my gold safely inside my boat. I've waited all my life for a score as big as this one . . . go ahead and shoot," he mocked. "No one is gonna take this from me now!"

"Fire!" came the command from the hilltop, and suddenly there were a dozen machine guns emptying their loaded magazines onto the dock and into the boat in the river below.

Jimmy underestimated the police. He dropped a box of gold on the dock and then dove into the black, cold water beneath the boat, hoping to elude the splaying bullets. He wasn't hit, but he had to hold his breath before he could safely surface on the other side of the boat for cover.

"All I need is just one more minute!" he thought, as he held his breath, swimming in long stokes beneath the surface. "If I raise my head for air, they'll certainly shoot me," he thought, just as he was beginning to pass out.

Eventually, he had to break the surface of the icy river to fill his aching lungs with air again. When he did, he saw from a safe distance that the police had taken his boat along with the millions of dollars' worth of his stolen gold.

"They probably think they killed me," he said to himself. "Ha! Someone should tell them what bad shots they are!" He treaded water until he watched the police finally leave. As he continued to tread water, he began to feel very tired, and was not sure how much longer he could do so, so he untied his boots and let them sink to the depths below. "That's better," he thought, but he still wasn't certain that he had the strength to swim all the way back to the dock. It seemed like a mile away. "They may have gotten my gold, but at least they didn't get me," he reasoned.

Suddenly, a small rowboat emerged from the mist, with a man standing in it, holding a long pole.

"Hey mister!" Jimmy cried, "pick me up and let me ride in your boat!"

The old man slowly steered his boat alongside Jimmy and helped him in.

"That's great old timer, now just get me to the other side as quickly as you can."

"The river is too wide and too deep to cross swiftly, and my evening on the river has tired my arms."

"Never mind that!" Jimmy replied angrily. "Just go as fast as you can. If I were not so exhausted, I'd row this boat myself!"

"As you wish," the old man sighed, "but why do you hurry so, and why are you out in the water so far from the shore?"

"Look, old man, if you only knew what I've been through tonight ... Just get us out of here and to the other side of the river. I'll take good care of you."

Jimmy was getting his breath back, and though he was beginning to feel more relaxed, he noticed that the mist had become a thick, dense fog. "How quiet the river has become," he said, looking over the port side of the boat to look for his reflection in the black water. "Hey! I think I see the shore, but it doesn't seem familiar." Jimmy thought that perhaps, the boat had drifted further down the river.

"We are not drifting, young man," the old man said. "There is no current in this river to take us anywhere other than to our destination."

Suddenly, the boat jerked as it hit the soft, muddy bank below it. Jimmy jumped out of the boat and climbing out of the water over the bar of sand, he said, "I have known this river all my life—ever since I was a kid—yet I don't recognize this beach."

Jimmy waited for an answer for a moment, and after not getting one, he turned around to the weary, old man, now seated in his boat with the long pole out of the water and resting across his lap.

"Don't you know who I am?" the old man asked. "I am Charon, the Ferryman of the underworld who transports the dead over the River Styx to the shores of Hell."

Worm Food

It was Friday night, and the library was closing. One by one, the section lights turned off. I always hated this part of my day when the library closed. If I could have my way, I would live 24x7 in the library, researching endless tomes of books on history and biography for my novels, a few of which I actually sold, though I was far from being a best seller. With a drinking problem and an artificial leg, no other work was available to me, so writing is how I earn my living, as meager and unrewarding as it is, financially speaking, that is.

With the librarian coughing at the door, suggesting that I hurry up and get out, I'd have to spend the rest of my evening in my cheap room across the street pouring over the notes that I culled from 30 hours of research I spent this past week in this old and damp library. If it were not already hard enough on me that I had a deadline by 4:00 tomorrow afternoon to turn in my manuscript so that I could get paid, I was going to get kicked out of my room for falling three weeks behind on my rent. I also owed the diner across the street, and Mrs. Ryan told me yesterday that she was going to cut me off until I gave her some money towards my tab. I told her that I expected to pay it off within the next couple of days, but she didn't seem to buy it. If I couldn't get any more meals from her until then, then it was going to be a long weekend. It would be vodka, sardines, and jam until I got paid for my story—if I even did.

I slept about five hours after my last edits of the manuscript, and since the diner below my boarding house opened at 6:00, I went down, and feeling like a low-life, I ordered a coffee and two eggs, over easy; hoping she wasn't thinking about my tab every five minutes.

"You heard about the grave desecrations, last night?" Mrs. Ryan asked me, slowly pouring coffee into a stained white coffee mug.

"No," I answered, pleasantly surprised that she was still serving me meals, in spite of her warning yesterday.

"That's right," she whispered, lowering her voice, "and the police were called to a desecrated grave early yesterday morning."

I spooned two or three teaspoons of sugar into my coffee and took a sip. It was still bitter as always, but it was what I needed to perk up.

"Here are your eggs," Mrs., Ryan said, sliding the yellow-stained, porcelain plate next to my coffee mug. "And don't forget about what we talked about yesterday, I need some money from you, or I'll have to cut you off. I'm sorry, Hon, but times are tough these days and I can't remain in business without folks paying for their meals. I know you're good for it, but I hope we understand each other."

"Absolutely, Mrs. Ryan," I said, wolfing down the eggs in two bites. "Tuesday, at the latest—I promise."

"Good," she said topping off my mug with more coffee.

"So," I said, looking over my shoulder at the empty diner, "not much of a crowd this morning, especially for a Saturday."

"Hmm," she barely acknowledged, leaning over her newspaper. "Who'd want to desecrate graves in this hick town?" she said to herself. "What do you reckon?" she said looking up to me over the rims of her spectacles.

"I have no idea," I said, sipping the hot, black brew. "It's an old town with a small grave yard, and a lot of the graves are more than 100 years old. What would be the point?"

"Listen to this," she said, snapping the paper open.

"'Desecration of Child's 100-year-old Grave.'"

"A child?"

"Can you believe it?" she said, reading on:

"'Whitehall, New Hampshire: At approximately 2:30 Friday morning, Rufus Bly, the sexton of the Hollis Street Church and Cemetery, was awakened by a ghastly scream. He investigated the area where he believed he heard it come from but found nothing out of the ordinary. He went back to sleep thinking it the result of a prankster. At 5:45, Bly began his morning rounds, and stepping through the Kellerman family plot, he was at once confronted with a pile of dark earth.

"'Upon further investigation, Bly discovered two small gravestones partially covered by the dirt, and a four-foot-deep hole in the ground beside the dirt pile. Next to the hole, a shovel was observed next to a pair of casket handles.

"'A pool of water filled half the hole, and inside the empty grave, a partially dug tunnel led toward a nearby plot. There was no casket to be found.

"'Early reports blamed the hole on animals, but the police have determined that, with the presence of a shovel, casket handles, and a missing casket, everything indicated the hole was manmade.

"''I don't believe they got what they were looking for,' Bly surmised. 'With all that water, and since the grave is almost 100 years old, there simply [isn't] much left, except maybe the skull.'

"'According to Dr. James Fox, the town's coronary officer, 'The skull is the last part of the skeletal remains to deteriorate with the erosion of water and other natural factors, simply due to its skeletal mass.'

"'The grave belonged to a five-year-old girl buried Christmas Day, 1920. Town records show that Garnet Kellerman passed away after a lengthy illness. Police believe the grave robber(s) may be members of a cult. Cults are known to believe that human skeletons particularly the skull holds special powers.

"'Hopewell sheriff, Fred Crane agrees. 'I don't believe there was much in there to begin with,' he said. 'The vandalism of this grave must have taken place recently, since the matted grass under the pushed over gravestone was green. That stone has not laid there for very long,' he speculated.

"'Dr. Fox said that the police will continue the investigation, and he believes it will produce a swift arrest, due to the abundance of evidence left at the grave site, not to mention what appears to be fresh blood at the site.'"

I tipped the last of my second mug of coffee to the back of my throat, and placing it down onto the counter, I looked into Mrs. Ryan's deep-set gray eyes and said, "now that's a story."

Sure enough, my agent came through with my check. I immediately paid off my rent and was eager to pay off my tab at the diner, which made Mrs. Ryan's old gray eyes sparkle with a hint of blue, a lingering trace from her younger days caught by a stream of light bursting through the faded yellow blinds of her front window.

"Be a hon, will ya, and open the blinds?" she asked.

As I twirled the blinds open, I caught a glimpse of an old man standing across the street. I had to take one of those "double-takes" because it almost seemed like he was looking directly at me.

I went outside to smoke a cigarette. There he stood, in a long black, thick wool coat and a large black fedora on his head. It was the middle of July and at 6:30 in the morning, it was already a humid 79 degrees. I took a few drags from my Marlboro cigarette and paced back and forth along the sidewalk, but each time I snuck a peak at this man across the street, he just stood there, with one hand deep in a coat pocket and the other holding a rolled-up newspaper.

As I squashed my cigarette into the sidewalk, he pulled his hand out of his pocket and motioned for me to cross the street to meet him on the other side.

I crossed the street. I was intrigued. As I approached him, I noticed that he was an incredibly old man, perhaps in his ninety's, judging from the deep furrows that plowed his leathery face and neck. My first thought was, where was his family or the men in white suits to allow such an old man to be out in this hot weather and wearing such heavy winter clothing. As I got closer to him, I noticed he had no ear lobes. He also had very brown eyes, almost black, like the kind of eyes you see from a dead fish.

Standing directly before him, I smelled something awful. I cannot explain it any other way. Not entirely disgusting, but it was something I noted immediately, and it was bothersome enough to cause me to step back a foot or two from him.

"I saw you," he said, with a raspy voice.

"Sir?" I pressed him.

"Over there. I saw you."

I assumed he meant that he noticed me across the street in front of the diner smoking a cigarette, but somehow, I was not so sure this is what he meant due to the way he said it, like he was sharing a secret with me.

He pulled out a piece of paper—yellowed newspaper. "I'm in need of someone to care for my property," he said, pulling a pencil stub from his coat pocket. He scribbled some numbers down, which I assumed was the phone number of his kids or the old folk's home that he escaped from.

He thrust it into my hand, but as he did, I noticed he had no thumb and that his fingers were webbed.

He saw that I noticed and smiled.

I put the paper into my trousers pocket, and turning around to cross the street, the rancid smell of the old man disappeared. On the other side of the street, I looked back, and the old man was gone! I looked to the left and to the right, but it was as though he completely disappeared. For a man in his advanced years, there was no way that he could have run away so quickly. I stood there, in front of Ryan's Diner, looking up and down the street and to the hill that rolled behind him, and nothing. It was as though he vanished in a moment, and it wasn't like he was picked up in a car, because I definitely would have heard it.

Reading my mail back at the apartment, my magazine article only bought me about two weeks of rent and board. I would have to start writing again. My agent told me that our publisher was tiring of the same old story lines and wanted something new and fresh. The implication was clear.

I spent the next week in the library, sourcing dozens of biographies, true crime articles, and other historical resources, but I could not concentrate. Did the recent grave consecrations and the appearance of this strange character have anything to do with each other? Why me? What would this black shrouded phantom want with me anyway?

Later that night, in the private filth of my cheap room, I removed my artificial leg and rubbed the aching stump with my hands. I had neglected it too long. The open sores were getting worse, and I found a few maggots that I quickly flicked off in disgust. It smelled terrible, ostensibly from the summer humidity and a possible infection. Though I could not afford it, I would eventually have to go back to the hospital and beg them to have more of my stump shaved off before sepsis set in. Leaning over closer to it, I could smell the infection, and then I suddenly made the connection with the putrid smell that I encountered with the strange dark man from nowhere.

"The paper!" I shouted aloud.

I frantically searched through the pockets of my pants and found the paper that the old man slipped me. I unraveled it and read, much to my astonishment, "Dec 25, 1920, Garnet Kellerman passed away to be with our Lord and Savior after weeks of illness. Memorial service will be held at the Kellerman family plot, Hollis Street Cemetery."

I crumpled the piece of yellowed newspaper into my fist in disbelief and tossed it into the trashcan. "Nothing made sense," I said to myself, as I poured a large glass of Vodka.

Hours later, I awoke from a drunken daze. I got dressed and assembled my artificial leg to my infected stump. Almost mad from pain, I swallowed another glass of Vodka and drove to the Hollis cemetery, but since the gate was locked, and wanting to avoid a confrontation with Bly, I found another entrance though a section of the gate that was missing. I eventually found the grave of Garnet Kellerman. The hole was still there.

To my astonishment, I saw a perfectly formed human leg lying at the bottom of the hole. It was muscular and smooth. I did not know what to make of this—it seemed like I was wide awake in some horrible nightmare—but there it was: a human leg—my leg! I climbed into the hole to get a better look at it, but when I looked up from the hole, I saw the old black phantom I had met earlier that day. Beside him stood a beautiful young girl.

"This leg is yours," the old man said in his raspy voice, but not until you feed my daughter, Garnet, with the worms from your rotting stump."

I looked at the leg lying at the bottom of the hole, and then up into the pleading eyes of the young girl. She stood beside the old man with her cadaver hands folded in front of her soiled dress, anticipating her rancid meal.

I paused for a brief moment and looked back down at my new leg lying in the hole. It was truly beautiful.

Lifting my head again, I focused on the cold, black eyes of the old man in black - not in fear, but with genuine excitement, and with sincere gratitude, I shouted, "Now HERE's a story!"

Twisted

He was tired.

With his hands on the wheel of his green '71 Plymouth Fury II, he cocked his head to the left and then to the right in an attempt to perk himself up. It was no use, so he turned on his AM radio, hoping some music might perk him up, but all he received was static. He looked over to his wife, sleeping soundly beside him. He was envious—he would do anything for an hour's nap. He looked at his wristwatch—4:30. It would be another hour before sunrise, when it would light up the dark ribbon of the seemingly endless highway before him, his eyes having become glued to it—mile after mile—a black and lifeless asphalt river without end.

He lit up the remaining stub of a cigar.

His wife woke up coughing, rolling down her window. "You know I can't breathe with your incessant smoking," she said, coughing into the slit of her window, continuing to roll it down as quickly as she could, "put out the heater!"

He cranked down his window and flung it outside, noting the chill of the fresh air as it flooded the car.

"We should have gotten a room in that last town," she said, coughing through the rolled-up fingers of her fist, but she knew that was not possible. The couple were on the lam, having ripped off "Big Tuna" Marella from his casino the night before.

Rain began to splatter against the windshield.

He switched on the wipers. They flicked back and forth, flinging water across the windshield without much effect. A few minutes later, he looked over at his wife, having fallen asleep again.

He fingered through the ashtray and pulled out a squashed cigarette. He and his wife were running for their lives, having made a huge score in gambling money skimmed off the top.

The rain stopped and just as the overcast sky began to yield to the sunlight creeping up over the Rocky Mountains in the distance, he noticed that the low fuel light was on. He figured he had another 10 miles before he ran out of gas. Lucky for him, a Shell station appeared six or seven miles later. He swung into the station beneath the blinking florescent lights of a rusted overhead tin carport roof and turned off the car.

"What'll you have?" the pale, pimpled-faced teen asked indignantly, pulling a soiled rag from his back pocket, wiping his greasy hands.

"Fill 'er up, Junior," the man said. "I'm going inside to get some cigarettes—'meet you back inside."

Through the static, a radio was playing country music inside the gas station. As he grabbed a carton of Camel's and a 6-pack of beer, the attendant walked into the station and parked himself before the antique cash register.

"OK, mister," he said, "that'll be twenty bucks for the gas, $5.00 for the carton of cigarettes and $2.50 for the beer. Anything else?"

"Gimmie a map," he said, opening his wallet.

Sure thing, Mr.," the kid said, slipping it into the brown paper bag.

"How far am I from Wildcat Falls?" the man asked.

"Maybe 50 miles," the attendant replied, over the annoying ringing of the old cash register. "You want a receipt?"

"Nah," the man said, sliding the paper bag of items under his arm. "Thanks."

"No problem," the kid said, slamming the cash register drawer.

The man let the screen door close behind him with a clanging of bells that were attached to it. He pulled out the map and looked over his shoulder to see if the kid was looking out the window. He was ready to blow his brains out if he was, fearing that he might have been recognized, but this was his guilty conscience working on him; no one reported him as a thief in any newspaper since he was an associate of the mob. It was the perfect crime, but still—it was a good thing this kid minded his own business, he thought.

He switched on the overhead light and unraveled the map across the steering wheel. His wife lifted her head from a deep sleep and strained her eyes under the gas station's bright flickering lights.

Where are we, Frank?" she yawned.

"About 50 or so miles away," he replied, lighting a cigarette. "Go back to sleep, it's gonna be another couple of hours. I'll wake you up just before we arrive. We'll get breakfast."

His wife turned away from him and settled deeper into the seat. His frown relaxed, and he immediately regretted the impatient tone in his response to her, pulling her cardigan up over her shoulders.

He started up the car and tossed the map onto the dashboard. Sitting back into his seat he braced himself for another long stretch of highway ahead of him. He floored the gas pedal, and with the sound of gravel flying from beneath the tires, he was soon back on the main road, guided by a single headlight.

The sun, no longer blotted by the horizon, yielded a panoramic view of gentle, pastoral hills. It quickly became humid, and Frank lowered his window to the smell of mown grass and the sound of his bald tires on wet asphalt. A cheerful glow of the red, morning sun filled his windshield.

Ninety minutes later, he nudged his sleeping wife awake and told her they were close to their destination.

She stretched and yawned, and then rolled down her window.

"Why does it get so humid after the rain?" she moaned, removing her sweater.

"It's the area," Frank responded, "it's a bit warmer in these parts."

They drove for another half hour, before Frank began to wonder if he'd missed the exit somewhere along the highway. They should have reached the town by now, he thought to himself.

After another 15 minutes, even his wife noticed that they appeared to be lost.

"Shouldn't we have come to the town by now?" she asked, fidgeting with her seat.

Frank lit up another cigarette and took a long drag. "I think I may have missed an exit off the main road. We definitely should have run into it by now."

He turned his car to the side of the road and cut the engine. Reaching for the map, he unfurled it, and tried to trace where he may have gotten off the beaten path.

"According to this map, the town should be right around here," he said, blowing smoke through his nostrils.

"How old is the map?" his wife asked, sarcastically.

"Well, it ain't *that* old!" he sniffed. "Seriously, according to this map, we should be in Wildcat Falls. I can't see how we missed it . . . strange . . . ."

He flicked his cigarette butt out the window and spotted a house on the other side of a large field.

"Let's go to that house over there and see if we can get some directions," he said, lighting up another cigarette.

"What house?" his wife asked, squinting her eyes for a better look.

"Over there!" he said, "it looks like a farm on the other side of this field."

"Whatever you say," she yielded. "Just get us there so we can get directions to a motel. My back is about to break from sitting in this lousy seat for so long."

Frank started the car and skid his tires on the soft earth until getting traction on the road with a squeal. His wife quietly ignored his profanity.

A few miles down the road, Frank said, "See?" pointing out of his window, "I told you it is a farm."

"Yes, I see it," his wife relented with a sigh.

When they reached the old, dark house, he cut the engine and got out of the car. The driveway was soft with mud caused by the rain the night before. In front of him, stood a large farmhouse. A farmer's porch was falling apart with rot. Brown, wet leaves were strewn all around it from the Autumn before. It didn't look like anyone had lived in the large house for a very long time. Across the driveway, a huge barn stood, leaning to one side with age. The yard and the nearby fields were overgrowth and unkept. The mailbox with flaking red paint was half-hanging from its post, mostly orange with years of rust. It was obvious that no one had been receiving mail for an exceptionally long time.

Frank climbed out of the car and tossed his sunglasses onto his seat through the open window.

"Go see if anyone is home," his wife urged him, leaning over the driver's seat.

"I doubt anyone's lived here for years," he said, burying his cigarette butt into the mud with the heel of his shoe.

He approached the farmhouse and noticed that the windows appeared to have been painted black. Perhaps someone still lived in this old place after all, since most buildings in this state of disrepair are missing most of their windows, but none of the windows of this farmhouse were smashed or missing—just painted black, for some odd reason.

"I'm going to knock on the door," Frank shouted to his wife from the porch.

He stepped up to the door, kicked away a pile of wet, rotted leaves that blocked it, and rapped on the stained-glass window that was fixed in the middle of it; a strange decoration for a farmhouse door, he thought. He stood there for a moment and then rapped on it again, only harder this time. He looked back at his wife with a shrug.

"Try the doorknob!" she shouted through the window of the car.

He tried to twist the doorknob, but the door was locked. He was about to turn away, when a frail young teenaged girl appeared from around the corner of the house in the shade of the overhead roof of the porch. He hadn't heard her approach, so when she appeared, he jumped, and embarrassed, he stepped back and attempted to explain his presence on her property. She was exceptionally beautiful, he thought, with the kind of beauty that can take a man's breath away. She was young and attractive, but with a very pale face. He noted the blue lines of blood vessels traversing across her brow, face, and neck. She wore kid gloves and a large, floppy hat, and she held a parasol close to her head.

"My wife and I are lost. I saw your house from the main road across the field. I'm sorry for imposing, but I—I mean, my wife and I—we were hoping you could point us in the direction of Wildcat Falls."

"You are in Littleton," she said, passively, almost in a whisper.

"I see," Frank said, thrusting a hand deep into his pants pocket, nervously fingering loose coins. "Would you be able to point us to a motel? We've been on the road for two days."

"You won't find a motel anywhere around here," she said.

There was a long, uncomfortable pause.

"Ask her if we can take a room!" his wife shouted. "We can pay for it!"

"Would this be possible?" Frank asked the strange girl.

"Anything is possible," she replied, with a slightly crooked smile, almost indiscernible. "We have plenty of room. Would you like to come in?"

"That sounds great," Frank said, pulling his hand out of his pocket and waving it to his wife to come to the house. "My wife and I are just exhausted. We'd be happy to pay you for a room just so that we can catch up on some sleep before we hit the road again."

"No money," she insisted, her voice startling Frank with its peculiar timbre. "No," she repeated, with a slightly higher voice, almost irritated. "We don't normally take in visitors or tourists, but I appreciate your situation. Keep your money, perhaps we can make this exception."

"We?" Frank asked. "Are there more of you—I mean, of your family?"

She passed in front of Frank, with a faint, unpleasant odor that he assumed was coming from her old clothes, and she opened the door as though it was never locked to begin with. Frank noted it with a confused frown that he shared with his wife, as she got out of the car. "That door was locked!" he thought to himself. She turned around and smiled at him mischievously, as though she had read his mind.

"Blanche!" Frank shouted to his wife, "get the suitcase and come on!"

The pale woman waited inside the front hallway with her hands behind her back, standing before an immense staircase directly behind her. Overhead there was a beautifully ornate chandelier. The morning sunlight cascaded through the stain-glass window of the half-opened door in a vibrant stream of colored light. Though mostly in shadows, the hallway was beautiful, charming, and inviting, Frank thought.

"Like I mentioned, we don't usually take in strangers," the woman said. "You are not from around here . . . are you?" she asked, almost regretfully.

"Perhaps my Bronx accent gave me away," Frank responded with a nervous chuckle.

The woman observed him silently, waiting for Frank's wife to enter the house.

"What a beautiful home," Blanche said, reaching out her hand to the woman. "It's so much more lovely inside compared to the outside," she said, before awkwardly realizing her gaffe. "I mean, your home—this house—it's so . . . it's so inviting."

The woman did not welcome Blanche's handshake, keeping her hands clasped behind her back, which Blanche thought a bit rude, especially when she was willing to pay their way.

"Are you sure there isn't a motel in the area?" Blanche asked. "We hate to intrude on you."

"You are not an intrusion, and there are no motels or other such accommodations for many miles, the woman said, in her monotone voice.

"Gather your things, and I will bring you to your room. You'll find it very comfortable."

Frank picked up their worn-out suitcase, and with his wife following close behind him, they followed the woman up the elaborate staircase. At the end of a long hallway on the second floor of the house, the woman opened a door to a large bedroom, complete with a huge, Victorian-era bed and a fireplace with a fire already going. She informed them that dinner was served late, at 8:00 in the evening, and she expected them to attend—promptly, with no exceptions.

"By all means," Frank assured her, noticing that all the windows in the bedroom were also painted black.

"There is a tray of cheese and wine. Help yourselves to it. You must be hungry."

As soon as Frank and his wife entered the bedroom, the young girl was gone.

"It's as though she was expecting us," Frank said. "Look at the cheese—it's fresh."

"And take a look at the fire," Blanche frowned, "and in this hot weather?"

"Hold on," Frank said. He walked to the fireplace and held his hands before it. "No heat!"

"What do you mean?" Blanche said with a mouthful of cheddar.

"Check this out!" Frank exclaimed with his hand in the fire itself. "Look at my hand! It's not burning . . . the fire isn't burning my hand . . . what is this?"

"Wake up, Frank," Blanche whispered into his ear. "It's already 6:30, can you believe it? We slept the whole day away and it's already dark!"

Frank rolled out of bed, reaching for a cigarette from the nightstand. "I'm famished," he said. "How about you?"

"We still have a while before dinner," his wife reminded him. "How about exploring this house? It's amazing!"

"Yeah, like that fire? I'm not crazy about this house, Blanche. I'm still freaking out over that fire thing." Frank lifted his head off the pillow and looked past his feet to the fireplace. "Looks like it went out. I need to ask her about this. Can you imagine how much that trick is worth? We could make millions! A fire year-round with no danger of burning, no heat, just a nice thing to look at. I need to talk to her about this."

"OK, OK," his wife pacified him, "but let's see what else is going on in this house."

"This is a private residence," Frank reminded his wife. "They are doing us a huge favor by letting us rest up before we continue our trip. The cheese snack this morning was great, but I'm so hungry, I could eat a Chinese doorknob."

"But aren't you the least bit interested, Hon?" she teased him. "That woman—white as a ghost—with all of that raven black hair falling down to her knees. She looks eighteen, but her presence and her mannerisms are of a much older woman. You heard her voice—a voice aged with maturity, and not of a teenage girl. There's something weird about her and this house—aren't you the least bit interested?"

"No."

"C'mon, Frank, don't be boring. Let's have a look around this mansion. This ain't no farmhouse, and you know it. This is a mansion of someone swimming in money. Look at this room! You saw the stain-glass window and the chandelier—what farmhouse do you know of that has such trappings? That woman was completely blind-sided by us, and it is obvious she's trying to placate us long enough to get us out of her hair. Don't ya get it? Am I the only one who sees this?"

Frank's unshaven face seemed calm and humorless in the warm light of the lamp.

"Listen," he said, firmly. "We're going to have dinner with these folks, go back to bed and get an early start in the morning for Wildcat Falls. If we do not hand over this money to Little Nicky by tomorrow, he's gonna put a hit out on us, if he hasn't done so already. Not to mention what the Big Tuna's got going on. We cannot remain in any one place longer than we absolutely need to."

"You're so boring!" his wife snapped.

Ten minutes to eight, Frank and his wife changed their clothes for dinner. The young woman who had invited them to lodge for the night knocked upon their door and then led them downstairs to the dining room, yet it was much more like the castle hall of an English Nobleman. It was immense, with a 20-foot-long oak table and a minstrel gallery at the far end of the cavernous room with ancient, tattered flags hanging down from the high ceiling. Frank recalled what his wife said earlier about the antiquated farmhouse being a cover for a wealthy man's estate. Perhaps she was right, he thought.

Twisted

The pale woman sat Frank and his wife at the long side of the table. Over the next few minutes, a dozen more people arrived, each taking their places at the table. No one introduced themselves, and there was no conversation, which Frank thought incredibly strange and very unnerving, since he and his wife were invited guests to dinner.

It was not until a very old man, regal in appearance, approached the head of the table and took his seat, when the others began to engage in conversation, yet Frank and his wife were completely ignored.

Frank was beginning to bristle from the uncomfortable situation. He pulled out a cigarette and was about to light it, but his wife caught his arm.

"Wait dear," she said quietly. "Don't draw attention to yourself—no one else is smoking. Let's get a good meal and then we can get out of here and hit the road again. I don't want to spend the night. I'm not comfortable. I think we got enough sleep."

This made good sense to Frank, so he relaxed, and put his cigarette packet away.

The old man at the end of the table seemed to be the patriarch of the family. He looked like he was ninety years old, with an ornate white mustache that covered his white, sharp teeth.

Frank suddenly recalled a book he read as an adolescent—"Dracula". It could not be possible, but here was a man, seated 12 feet away from him who had all of the attributes of the villain from Bram Stoker's early chapters of the novel when Harker first encounters the aged Count.

In an attempt to make conversation, Frank said, "I'm sorry, Sir, but you look just like the description of the vampire from Stoker's classic horror story." This certainly seemed to break the ice, because now all eyes focused on Frank. He leaned over his place at the table, and looking all around it, he said, "this place is starting to make sense to me now," lighting his cigarette after all. "In fact, I'll bet all of you are vampires."

The pale young woman approached Frank and his wife with her long fangs barred and saliva dripping out of the corners of her mouth, and said, "Yes, Frank, we are vampires, but we are ladies and gentlemen first, unlike you and your wife.

"I invited you into our home, which is much different than when you mortals invite us into your homes. When you invite us into your homes, it is typically for selfish reasons, so we overcome you and destroy you—with pleasure I might add—but when we invite mortals into our home, even as irascible as you and your wife are—to dine at our honorable table, to sleep in our noble bedrooms—we are honor-bound to protect you.

"Unlike you mortals, we treat you with respect as honored guests. So, you are free to dine at our table to get your strength back and sleep soundly and safely in the bedroom we provided you with, but before the sun rises tomorrow, you best be on your way before something worse happens to you."

The next morning just before the rising of the sun, Frank and his wife were back on the road, and if it was even possible for hardened criminals, like them, they were a little wiser than they were the day before.

Second Sight

Journal of Dr. Jonathan Sinclair, PhD Psychology, Parapsychology

JUNE 10, 1977:

I was visited by a woman with her 19-year-old daughter, who claims-she is "seeing things", such that these apparitions are causing a significant disruption in the family and with her attendance at college. When pressed for examples, she said that her daughter is highly creative: painting, music, poetry, obsessed with photography, etc.

Note: *Patient is currently on high blood pressure medication, a blood thinner and two anti-depressants. Non-smoker, non-drinker, morbidly obese.*

One example she gave involved a family trip they made to the Grand Canyon last year. During this vacation, the family spent a day at "Circus, Circus," Las Vegas, visiting the waterpark. At some point the husband left his wife and son at the waterpark and took his daughter with him into the casino, where he played several hands of blackjack and tried his luck at the slot machines.

Not winning any money in these games of chance, he decided to place a few bets playing roulette on their way out. After a placing the bets, and still not winning any money, he decided to count his loses and leave, but his daughter suggested he place a bet on #17, which he did as a lark. When the ball landed on #17, her father shouted with surprise and hugged his daughter, overcome with excitement. After he cashed in his chips, having won his money back plus forty dollars more, his daughter suggested he try it again, only to make an additional outside bet by placing some chips on the black square. Her father complied, placing half his chips on #17 and the other half on black. To his surprise, he won again. Overcome from his unexpected fortune, he asked his daughter if he should continue, to which she told him to wait until three more rolls completed, and then to bet on #17 and black again. He contemplated keeping some of the chips back for himself so that he would at least leave the casino in the red in the probable event that he would lose, but his daughter told him that unless he bet everything he had already won from the casino, he'd lose everything. Not batting an eye at this unusual response by his daughter, he decided to follow her advice, and again, he won both bets, making him a few thousand dollars richer—almost enough to pay for the vacation.

"Should I make another bet?" he asked her, but she said she "couldn't see anymore." Not understanding what she meant, he decided to cash out anyway, considering he was on the upside of his day in the casino.

Another example she provided took place at college. As a first-year student, she hadn't made any meaningful friendships, except for a connection she had with a young man in his sophomore year. The woman made it clear that there was no romantic connection between her daughter and this young man, but they both shared an interest in art, having met in an art class.

After three or four weeks developing a purely platonic relationship, they decided to take their paint kits to the country and spend the day painting together.

As the day was losing its light, they packed up and headed back to his car. Along the way, she experienced a flashing manifestation of brilliant light. He asked her what the issue was, and she suggested they wait a few minutes for her to regain her composure before continuing their walk back. Perplexed be her response, her painting partner placated her, not wanting to further upset her. After a short break, she said she felt better, and they continued their walk back to the car. When they reached it, all of the windows of his car were smashed from someone throwing large rocks at it and one of his tires was flattened. He noticed the footprints in the area indicated more than one person was involved.

The next day in the papers, there was a report of four men having been arrested for assaulting another couple in that very area. This event caused the young man to discontinue his relationship with her daughter, which has since caused her a tremendous amount of grief.

I told the woman that I would be willing to see her daughter and had my secretary provide her with an appointment.

Note: *probable eidetic capability.*

June 21, 1977:

Met with the young woman, whom I will refer to as "Jane." Nineteen years old, timid, introverted, intelligent, passionately creative.

After spending an hour with this patient, I believe she is dealing with eidetic memory. She can see objects hours (or, in some cases days) after the light-source is cut off or the object is no longer available. These "after images" or "intuitive images" are as optically vivid to her as when first seen or experienced. Typically, this form of perception is more generally found in childhood, where it disappears with the onset of puberty. In some cases, this phenomenon, sometimes referred to as a mediumistic gift, can continue into adulthood, as it appears to be the case with Jane. I have seen such cases in persons with advanced age and in almost all of them, such persons are retained to artists, persons with heightened sensitivity, or, in instances where the patient is a geriatric, it may be due to heredity or environment. North Germany has the highest reports of such examples, though my research does not explain why.

Responses to my questions indicate a troubled young woman. She admits to bouts of depression but is unable to provide reasons for the melancholia. She experiences horrific nightmares such that she delays sleep, which explains the dark rings under her eyes and a sort of listlessness she exhibits. She admits to hearing "tapping's" and "voices," especially when she is the most tired from lack of sleep. Other dreams are extremely vivid such that when she awakens, she continues to act out the dream in reality.

Note: *her mother attested to this.*

She acknowledges an unusual relationship with apparitions, or ghosts, which she says began at four years of age. When I asked her for an example, she said that there are times when she hears "strange noises strange noises." Sometimes these noises become voices, but this was on rare occasions. When I asked her what the voices were saying, she replied that she can never remember the actual words, but she remembers how the voices made her feel, such as feelings of inadequacy and incompetence in her interests and affairs. [**Note:** malevolent spirits?]

When further pressed, she said that the voices start out as whistling—the kinds of tunes that little children sing together—but lately the shrill tunes seem like funeral dirges, and she wanted them to stop bothering her. She also stated that she has become accustomed to using charms to help diminish her sufferings, but that they are apparently inadequate to provide any measurable relief, hence seeking my help through her mother.

June 28, 1977

In order to understand the degree of Jane's eidetic vision and the categories they fall into, namely, her mood swings leaning on melancholy, hearing noises/voices, nightmares, vivid dreams and appearances of light, ghostly apparitions, excursion of the soul, and mediumistic gifts, I will break these down on subsequent appointments to evaluate treatment.

I asked Jane which of these categories she would like to handle first, and she chose nightmares. I asked how often she had them and she said that although she dreams vividly most nights during sleep, the dreams gradually became darker during the waxing phase of the moon, with the worst dreams occurring during the full moon. She also said that her visions can happen any time during the day, but they are the most vivid and "real, life-like" in the nightmares she endures during the full moon. I looked up her birthdate (10/27/1958) in a lunar calendar and found that she was born during the full moon phase.

Note: *Visions and nightmares during the brightest lunar phase are most pronounced in persons who struggle during childhood with certain ailments related to the neck, vocal cords, throat, and thyroid gland during a full moon that do NOT require surgery. In such cases, the child is either prayed over via Christian/Judeo beliefs or charmed via spiritual seances or conjuration. Jane's mother informed me that her daughter had a tonsillectomy when she was five. When I pressed her on her religious/occult practices at that time, she further told me that her family was not associated with the church, but that her grandfather was a diviner. However, though her grandfather was aware of his great-granddaughter's medical situation, she was not aware of any mystical intervention from him; he would not* *have mentioned it and she never thought to ask him. Noteworthy is her grandfather was of North German descent.*

I asked for examples of her nightmares:

A typical nightmare may involve a series of the same vision—beginning with the brighter waxing phase leading up to the full moon—and these types of nightmares always involve her death. For instance, on the first night, she will be walking through a dark house, and though she is alone, she feels like someone is leading her somewhere. When she sees a casket in the distance, she wakes up perspiring heavily and gasping for breath [**Note**: check medical history for apnea]. On each subsequent night, she gets closer and closer to the casket and by the night of the full moon, she is being shown the top of the casket where the lid is removed, and she finds herself dead in the casket and with her neck slit ear to ear [**Note**: a vision related to the neck!].

She has especially frightening, recurring nightmares of being hunted and eaten alive—or running from—either a bear or a shark (but never by both).

She dies and awakens in a strange dimension ("another world" she called it).

She shared one of her most terrifying nightmares with me, a recent one, which is a good example of the 'vividness' she tried to explain:

"I was speeding on a long winding road through hills and along cliffs that towered over the crashing waves of the Pacific below. It was raining hard. I had too much to drink. I was in a hurry to get home and I unintentionally cut someone off, and now he was after me in a fit of road rage. I had difficulty looking through the windshield of my dark blue Corvair because it was fogging up with my anxious breath.

"I lost control and the car careened over the edge of the winding road and down to the rocks and the raging surf below. Suddenly, I found myself transported from my leather seat to above and outside my car. From one moment, I was an observer from above during the chase, and the next moment, I was in my car after it crashed and blew up into a ball of fire. I seemed to bounce back and forth from reality and another abstract dimension.

"I remember thinking, 'Am I watching myself die?'

"After the car rolled over and over down the rocky cliff, it settled into a funeral-like pyre. There were a few peaceful moments of what felt to me like a kind of drifting. In retrospect, I would say my soul was detaching from my dead, scorched body and somehow continued to hover over the incident, but I was confused by what was happening.

"In a flash, I found myself in a desert terrain at night. To my left, there was a sort of white-washed structure with a welcoming light emanating from an open door. Beyond me there was what appeared to be the last remaining moments of an orange glow of a sunset, only there was no sun.

"A very tall, handsome, bald man walked out of this door and stood before me. He appeared to be in his thirty's. He wore a loose, white garment with the sleeves ending at the elbows and with a kind of skirt that covered his legs just above his knees. He stood before me and placed his open palms together. I think he was barefooted.

"I had not even taken notice of my own condition at this point. I was merely an observer in a state of shock, but when he stood before me in such a mild, calm manner, I looked at myself and saw that I was similarly dressed. I cannot explain why, but this seemed to settle me down.

"He told me to get down on my knees and to outstretch my hands—palms down on either side of me, which I did without hesitation. I wanted to ask him where I was, but I found that I had no ability to speak. Perhaps it was the shock of it all . . .

"From this position, you will lower your head and raise your left hand to form a "C" with your fingers and thumb, bringing it in front of your face. You will then do the same with your right hand, so that you will end up forming a circle around the center of your mouth. You will hold this position until told to do otherwise."

"I suddenly found my tongue and asked him if I should do as he instructed, to which he replied that I should.

"'Keep your head down,'" he repeated, as I had momentarily looked up to him for his approval. "'You are not to make eye-contact.'"

"Since there was no sign of fire, or of devils, I assumed I was being inducted into a heavenly state. Though I was not born into a Christian family, my parents tried to raise me with good principles and morals. We attended a church service every Easter and Christmas and I was even baptized as an infant. Though I strayed from the morality they taught me at times throughout my life, I always returned to the morals my parents tried to instill in me. I have always been a good person. I tried to live a good life. I never hurt anyone. I did not judge anyone. Was this apparition that stood before me my eternal judge? Was he an angel that was about to cast me into the Lake of Fire or was he preparing me to present myself before the Lord God Almighty Himself?

"By now, I knew that I was dead. So far, I sensed that I was in a good place. The tall man was kind, though he did not smile. I was confused by his instructions, but I sensed that it was for my own good.

"He asked me to practice this strange sort of choreography. At first, I could not seem to get it right, but after some time, he was convinced that I was finally capable of remembering this series of movements, almost like a dance.

"He stretched out his hand. I placed mine into his and I felt reassurance—almost a sense of pleasure—until he tightened his grip and said, '''Do not forget this.''' Then he lifted my chin to lock eyes with his and repeated more firmly, '''Do NOT forget this.'''

"I asked him when I would need to take this position, and he simply replied, '''You will know.'''

"He beckoned for me to stand up and join him as the door opened and a flood of light blinded his presence from me. He reached out his huge hand again and though I could only feel it on my shoulder, I submissively permitted him to guide me in through the door, which closed behind us, but then he was gone. I never saw him again.

"I found myself in a sort of hallway. The light was warm, and it made me feel safe and secure like the days of my youth when sitting before the fireplace on so many Christmas Eves, surrounded by laughter and singing. I had no idea what to do next, so I decided to walk toward the light ahead, which seemed to brighten and expand with each step I took. Was this "the light" that everyone talks about when they recall their near-death experiences? I then realized that I seemed to have some sort of body, yet there was a transparency to it. When I walked toward the light, I could feel my body moving but I could not feel the ground with my feet.

"At some point, I reached another door that seemed to block all of the splintered light from this massive beam. I thought it would nearly blind me if I could not look away from it, and I found that I was unable to.

"I waited for a long time, and with no movement or sound from or beyond the door, I rapped on it with my hand, yet there was no feeling in my hand. I heard the sound of flesh knocking on wood, but I had no sense in my hand to indicate that it was actually connecting with the door—assuming it was physical to begin with.

"The door opened, and a dozen beautiful faces suddenly appeared and beckoned me in.

"My first thought was that I had to be in heaven. So much light. Such care by the man I initially met outside, and now all of these beautiful, young smiling faces surrounding me from all sides to enter through the door, which I did.

"As soon as I passed through the door, I smelled the slightest whiff of something wrong. It was not particularly a bad odor, but it smelled of the slightest scents of impurity, like when milk has turned sour. However, this was quickly spirited away when I noticed the diversity of the faces of these young people. They were both male and female, and all in their late teens or early twenties.

"All of a sudden, I found myself with a physical body. The hair that had burned up in the fire, returned. My body appeared as it was before the crash, only I was no longer overweight; I was slender and voluptuous. The men and woman that greeted me had very bright eyes and broad smiles, each one of them placing their hands on me in a welcoming gesture, almost as though to give me their blessings.

"One of the men, with long brown hair, a dense beard and clear green eyes approached me from the back of this welcome committee of sorts. The group made way for him to approach me and as he did, I noticed that everyone else had slowly—almost sheepishly—disappeared into the background."

"'I'm Michael,'" he said, with a smile. "'Welcome.'"

"I did not know how to respond—or if I even should. I nodded my head in respect and nervously waited for his next words."

"'You are in a very good place,'" he said, his smile lowering. "'As you can see this is a happy place . . .'"

"'Unless you fail!'" a young man said, from the far side of the cavernous room.

"When I heard this, I was immediately overcome with uncertainty because if I was in Heaven, there is no room for failure. I cannot express to you how upsetting this was to me, and so it was at this point when the dream splintered off into a nightmare.

"Alarmed, I said, "'What does he mean?'"

"Michael told me to ignore the man, as he slung his heavy arm over my shoulder.

"He led me into a smaller room off the large, cavernous hall, and once inside, it looked to me like a beautiful kitchen . . . sinks, ovens, stovetops, cooking utensils, and plates . . . but no refrigerators for meats, vegetables, and no cabinets for seasonings, which I found odd. In fact, this experience was beginning to perplex to me—more so than the negative comment uttered a moment before. Looking in all directions of the pristinely sterilized galley, I began to believe that I was, perhaps, not in Heaven, but in Purgatory.

"'You were taught the form?'" Michael asked me, gently.

"Assuming he meant the series of positions I was shown outside in the desert, I replied, "'Yes.'"

"'Do NOT forget them,'" he said, with his clear green eyes boring a hole into mine.

"'Why,'" I asked. "'When would I have any use of using it?'"

"'You will know,'" he answered stoically, and then he was gone as quickly as the tall man who met me outside in the desert.

"I found myself alone in this brightly lit, steel-clad, professionally furnished kitchen, when a young man in his early twenty's walked in. I assumed he was the chef. He smiled, like they all do so easily, yet without warmth. "'You are new here,'" he said, almost smirking.

"For the first time, I seriously thought that, perhaps, I was not in a heavenly place after all, but that I was somehow sanctioned for the place of unspeakable terrors. I began to hope that this was at least Purgatory and not Hell. I was too uncertain to believe it, since I was unable to accept such a possibility, but with each passing moment, I found myself wrestling with this progressive experience growing with cynicism, insincerity and what seemed like spiteful hypocrisy.

"I looked out through the kitchen door and all the people who met me earlier were gone. Off in the distance, I saw Michael sitting behind a tall narrow desk, similar to a podium. Our eyes met, but his brows furrowed with indignation before he quickly looked away.

"'What happened to all of the nice people?'" I asked the young man.

"'Now that they've served their master, they have returned to their work,'" he said, his smirk slowly fading.

"'Their master?'" I asked.

"'We all have our masters,'" he said, "'but I've said too much!'"

"'I don't understand,'" I said, with my heart falling with each minute of this conversation.

"'Right now, there is relative peace. It's been over 300 years since I've last been ravaged by my own master,'" he said, "'but when my master confronts me, the agony is beyond imagination and the cruelty is ferocious and lingering.'"

"'What do you mean by your master? Are there others?'"

"'Each of us have several masters,'" he said, leaning against a wall. "'They tend to leave us alone unless we do something to irritate them, and when we do, you will truly wish you were never born.'"

"'So, this is not Heaven?'" I asked faintly.

"The young man—whose name was never offered to me—threw his pock-marked face back and laughed with contempt at my innocent, yet reasonable question.

"'Oh, I must be quiet . . . I do not want to wake the master. The last time he confronted me, it took many years to get my form back, as you behold it now. Also, now that you are rightfully his, you must be quiet, you must be clever and do everything to avoid a confrontation. Even one confrontation with him every hundred years or so will take what seems like twice as long for you to recompose.'"

"As he spoke, I began to feel increasingly isolated. There were no friends here. No comforts. No escapes. As I contemplated such things, I tripped and caused a drawer of utensils to fall to the floor.

"'Better take care,'" the young man said. "'Though it has been a long time since an interaction with the ancient one, a noise such as this might possibly arouse him, and with you being new here . . .'"

"Suddenly, a scream such as one that could only emanate from 1000 anguished souls filled the room, and in a second, I threw myself to the floor in the position taught to me ('you will know when to use it').

"I closed my eyes, but my new eternal body could not shield me from the forthcoming horrors that were about to unfold without the need to see.

"I cannot fully describe the demon that appeared without fainting from sheer horror, but it was about four feet high and covered in hair. It hopped on a single spidery leg. In the middle of its head, there were huge teeth in various shapes and sizes and from each side, two large hands, each with three long talons.

"I immediately took the position on the floor in total submission and as I slid my hands palms down to either side of my trembling body, I suddenly felt the creature—almost gently—place its grotesque hand over mine as if to stop me from completing the form. As I froze in place, I was then subjected to hours of this creature tearing apart this man, and as far as I could tell, consuming him slowly as one did when enjoying the delicacies of the former world. The man's screams for mercy went unheeded and I had to wonder when the beast would turn on me. Yet it did not.

"When it was all over, the beast transformed itself into the most beautiful image of a man as I have ever seen. It told me that his name was 'Legion', since he himself already had one thousand lower ranking demons raging inside of him, gnawing at him like eternal pests day and night. Behind him were the remains of the young man, though apart from the blood splattered all over the kitchen, there was not much of him left. I wondered why there was blood, having previously assumed we were of a celestial, spirit-like form.

"I continued to hold my position on the floor, shaking uncontrollably from stark-raving fear.

"'Did you believe at first you were in Heaven?'" it asked.

"'I did.'"

"'Like so many, you will be in Heaven for twenty minutes before the devil knows you're dead. You are now the master of my kitchen,'" he said, in the most calm and reassuring voice. "'Hopefully, we will not need to chastise you. Millions of years living in fear is hell enough but crossing us will seem like an eternal death in hell. Most recover, but there are some who do not.'"

"With this, the demon pulled what looked like a ball of light from the splattered blood and gore on the wall, and he swallowed it whole.

"'He is one of us now,'" he said. "'Be certain that you are not next to join him.'"

"Not knowing what to do next, I continued the movements of the form and made the circle with my hands before my face, as I was taught.

"'You've done well,'" he said, "'but next time, and there may never be a next time, but if there is, and if I happen to be in the mood, you must make the circle in front of your mouth.'"

"Suddenly, he was gone, and I was left alone to contemplate my eternal destiny for such a wasted, useless life."

I asked her how these nightmares made her feel; how they affected her during the day. She said they made her very depressed (another one of the key categories of one who suffers with eidetic memory). I asked how she handled her depression and she said that she was on iproniazid, a monoamine-oxidase inhibitor that had been used in the treatment of tuberculosis, and imipramine, the first drug in the 1950's in the tricyclic antidepressant family to be prescribed for depression.

Note: *I took Jane off her two current anti-depressants and put her on a tetracyclic one. Follow up in two weeks.*

July 12, 1977:

The TeCA med appears to work better with Jane. When I asked for her mother's opinion, she agreed, and though this change in medication therapy has not adversely impacted her dreams, she reported that the vividness of them seemed to lessen (slight improvement). However, this is more likely due to the waning lunar cycle (new moon on July 16).

Note: *follow up with appointment after the next full moon, 7/30 to evaluate effectiveness of drug changes.*

I asked Jane about the "noises" she hears at times. She said that the noise typically begins with a shrill sound and may last for seconds or minutes, sometimes escalating into what she perceives are voices, though she cannot decipher actual words from the chatter. She said it sounds like "a crowd of people whispering." I also asked her about the tapping sounds she hears on occasion, especially when she is about to fall asleep.

Her perception of these audible interferences belong to both an eidetic memory and subjection to the occult. I have ruled out a direct occult influence since neither mother nor daughter practice an involvement with the occult, but I recall Jane's great-grandfather, who was known by the family for his mediumistic gifts, such as moving chairs and fortune telling. This means that there remains at least an occultic *influence*, which I believe is still quite strong based on my interviews with Jane over the last four and a half weeks.

I asked her how she handled these intermittent audible interruptions and she replied that she had become accustomed to them since she first started experiencing this phenomenon as far back as she can remember (earliest recollection, 4 years of age). It was not until she started attending public school in the first grade when she learned that no one else experienced such sensations.

Her parents had her evaluated by an ENT physician when she was approximately seven years old, but no inner ear abnormalities were detected. When she was eleven years of age, she was evaluated by a mental health clinician. Aside from her complaint of nondescript acoustic manifestations, which she refers to as "noise," he found none of the typical behaviors related to schizophrenia or other mental illnesses. This makes sense to me because such visionaries are not by any means persons who are incapable of coping with normal realities. Hence, without a meaningful diagnosis which would point to either a physical or a mental issue, they eventually accepted that Jane was "gifted" and that this sensation was something that did not pose a threat to her overall health and well-being, since she was not actually hearing distinct words emanating from this "noise." They also considered that this "noise" was likely something she would grow out of, not having any other alternatives available to uncover the source [of what I found to be at least one of the six categories associated with eidetic memory].

Note: Jane has experienced all six known categories of eidetic memory, with "excursion of the soul" being her most recent experience.

1. *Melancholy/Depression*
2. *Nightmares/Vivid Dreams*
3. *Sounds/Voices*
4. *Appearances of light/optical manifestations of past memories*
5. *Excursion of the soul*
6. *Mediumistic gifts*

    P.S.: research 'hereditary transmission' of eidetic ability.

August 5, 1977:

I followed up with Jane's nightmares and melancholy moods following the full moon of July 30. She stated that there was no change in the intensity of her nightmares since our last appointment but indicated her mood has improved with less anxiety/depression and that there was a noticeable reduction in the frequency of the audible attacks of what she continues to refer to as "[background] noise" and "whispering voices."

This is promising progress, but the medication only provides relief on a temporary basis. I am certain that once the medication is stopped, these symptoms of an eidetic memory will return.

I will continue the drug therapy as it is managing these symptoms, but I am beginning to believe that this is more of a spiritual issue than a physical and/or mental health issue at work.

Note: *[Reviewed Case #'s 116, 123, 222, 302, 312, 444]*

A couple of examples from my casebook indicates these patients experienced at least one of the six categories of an eidetic memory:

A Christian missionary pilot ("Peter") complains of nightmares and audible sounds that only he can hear. When serving in the Sambia tribal territory of Papua New Guinea, he and two fellow missionaries returned to a village where they shared the message of the Holy Bible. The purpose of the flight was to bring translated versions of the New Testament and medicines. The chief of one of these tribes had converted to Christianity, as well as much of his tribe. One member of the tribe, their shaman, rejected the missionaries as hostile and would have nothing to do with them or the converted members of the tribe. When this pilot asked for a meeting with the shaman in an attempt to convert him, the old shaman agreed, much to the delight of the missionaries. However, during this meeting, the shaman told them that the reason he did have any interest in their 'black books and medicines' was because he was already the healer for the tribe's various illnesses and other afflictions, as was his father before him, and his father before him. The pilot asked him why he held such animosity for the Gospel message, and he replied that he could prove his powers were as potent as "this God you teach" and offered an example. The pilot and his two friends were intrigued.

Second Sight

The shaman closed his eyes and proceeded to tell them exactly what lay over the hills and mountains—many miles from their village. He told them about the rivers that traversed through the rain forest and jungles and also gave their locations relative to the lay of the land. He told them about the other villages that he could see and gave them the locations of each one. He called this gift, "second sight."

When he opened his eyes, the three men were astounded. Checking his maps, the pilot confirmed that the shaman was 100% accurate. The fascinating factor of what this shaman shared with these men was that he had never set foot outside the tribal village all of his life, and no one from the tribe had ever ventured into the rain forest more than a mile from the center of their small village. When his two friends looked at the pilot for acknowledgement, he responded that he himself had seen everything the shaman had seen in his vision from the many flights he logged as part of his job.

When this pilot retuned to the states for a furlough, he began to suffer piercing audible sounds that he compared to someone running their fingernails across a chalkboard. On top of this, he also endured terrifying, vivid nightmares. He assumed the shaman had cursed him, which he thought made sense, since he was attempting to supplant this powerful old man's authority over the tribe with the authority of a foreign religion.

He also told me about a new ability he seemed to acquire since that trip—what he referred to as getting 'peeks into the future.' For instance, seeing a glass fall from a table and having his hand ready to catch it.

I explained to him that he was experiencing a mediumistic gift, more than a curse, though I was not ready to rule out the possibility that the shaman had indeed proclaimed a malevolent curse over him, considering the nightmares and audio nuisance from which he was suffering. I told him that he could explore his mediumistic gift of clairvoyance or renounce it. He opted to be free of it, so I recommended that he visit his pastor or priest in order to exorcise it from him, which is the course of action he decided on. Having not heard from him since, I suspect he followed through with the religious option for a cure.

Another patient ("Debra") claims that, with concentration, she has the ability to summon any deceased person known to her. With this powerful mediumistic gift, she stated that she could use it to make a comfortable living as a medium in seances. In the realm of perception, the characteristic relationship between an eidetic memory and spiritism (i.e., "astral bodies," "aura," "mystical separation," etc.) begs the relationship of synaesthetic apparitions to the corresponding occult experience. At this level, the priority of psychological or psychical research may be usurped by the psychological disorders that are most associated with this phenomenon and their cure. In my opinion, I see both eidetic and occult activity on the same level as it relates to mediumistic gifts, the difference between the two being, eidetic memory seems to be a spiritual affliction, whereas divination can be abandoned by the practitioner at will, such as with Debra who, realizing she could make a good income as a medium, chose instead to deny it in her pursuit of charismatic gifts (laying on of hands, speaking in tongues, prayer, etc.).

Another patient ("Richard") complained of vivid dreams (though not nightmares) and sudden appearances of light at different times during consciousness. On several occasions, he thought he saw "angelic-like figures" in these flashes of light. Other times, he would be visited by a memory, such as in one example, when he was shown a quick replay of himself running on a playground with several other children. He said that he dreamed vividly from his youth, and as early as four or five years of age he saw "colored circles." By the time he was thirteen, flashes of light started to manifest at inconvenient times during the day, such as being in a classroom situation in school. Upon further interviewing of Richard, he revealed that his mother was a palm-reader and had what seemed to him a gift of clairvoyance. He also witnessed her lifting a kitchen table one time, merely from concentration. When he was twelve, he contracted mononucleosis (**Note**: throat related ailment: sore throat, swollen lymph nodes . . .) which tuned into Guillain-Barré syndrome and landed him in the intensive care unit for two and a half weeks. As a charmer, his mother "healed" him, as she may have done all through his childhood, perhaps beginning when he was an infant. Soon after his thirteenth birthday, he developed acoustic manifestations and visions. In Richard's case, there is a clear eidetic disposition that has its roots in the direct occult activities of a parent.

Note: Jane's great-grandfather's divination and Jane's eidetic memory:
I see that occult activity may be the cause, and eidetic predisposition its offspring. Jane's heeding of special signs using fetishes/charms is based on her belief that "second sight" is dependent on some special

hour or day, such as Christmas Day, midnight at the New Year, the hour of one's birth, etc. (see entry from June 21). As opposed to eidetic memory, "second sight' is comprised of several mediumistic gifts, such as reading tea leaves, cards, and palms. This is where the boundary becomes obscured when attempting to compare eidetic and superstitious/magical gifts/practices. If there is a spirit behind eidetic memory as there certainly is behind divination, then all the psychiatry in the world cannot cure one who suffers from eidetic memory, since it does not appear to be a gift, or if it is, it seems to me a mixed blessing because it does not benefit the host as does, perhaps, the ability to prophesy.

The burden of eidetic memory does have its benefits, but only from the individual's perspective. For instance, seeing a past memory in a momentary flash of light may be a pleasant experience—assuming the past memory was a good one—but it only benefits the individual. Mediumistic gifts, such as palm reading, benefit both the practitioner (financially) and the customer (he or she walks away with a good fortune, or if it is not "in the cards," so to speak (s)he can takes steps to improve their future by manipulation of their actions.

With respect to the relationship between Jane and her great-grandfather, there can be no doubt as to the connection between eidetic and occult involvement and subjection. Eidetic ability is a secondary effect of divination. Persons who, as children were charmed in cases of illness, such as Jane's great-grandfather's magic conjuration during her tonsillectomy as a child, grow into adulthood with a development of "second sight."

In conclusion, eidetic ability in adults—apart from artistic, creative, or passive/intuitive visions—may be a mediumistic gift, though not as clairvoyance is. Nonetheless, it may be at least conditioned by occult participation as 'hereditary transmission.'

August 12, 1977:

This is where my association with Jane becomes interesting. I mentioned the eidetic category of the excursion of the soul with her after deducing her eidetic memory is likely the result of her relationship to her great-grandfather. She confirmed that she has at times—during periods of "feeling good"—been able to leave her body and visit distant places (see notes from August 5, example #1). The significance of this finding is that her eidetic memory is a direct result of her great-grandfather's involvement in the occult. This is a breakthrough for me because now there is a path to curing her.

She provided several examples of this phenomenon, which make it clear that she has this mediumistic gift. It is the only category of eidetic memory that is not a problem for her, such as the acoustic and optical manifestations are. I asked her if she used this gift to escape the other more problematic categories and she responded by saying that she leaves her body when the other categories are either minimal or not present at all. The reason being is when she attempts to escape the "noise" for example, the "noise" follows. Hence, it only made sense to leave her body when she was "feeling normal."

As far as a cure is concerned, I gave her examples of former patients of mine that were successful in rejecting their mediumistic gifts in order to be free from them (August 5, #2). She found this problematic: as much as she dislikes the nightmares, "noise" and light manifestations, she would find it difficult to give up the ability to leave her body, where she has visited distant lands with great pleasure.

I explained that it was an "all or nothing" cure. Either she reject all mediumistic gifts in order to be liberated from the ones that cause her suffering, or she continue to keep all of them if she wants to continue deploying excursions of the soul. Instead of being happy and relieved at the prospect of not having to be subjected to depressions and vivid nightmares, for instance, she said that she would need time to consider her options. Such is the pull to be able to leave the body when she desired to. We agreed to meet again in two weeks.

Note: excursion of the soul does not appear to be a splitting of the ego, but instead, a mystical capability of the mind having the power to send the soul out of the body and visit other places in the world on command. The brain does not appear to be strong enough to be able to withstand these supernatural/spiritual powers, which I believe are alien to our bodies and souls, since so few people truly have them.

I have examples of patients who have accepted their mediumistic powers as "gifts from God." However, I disagree with this premise since so many of these patients, 1) seek a cure, or a release from the grips of these powers, 2) opens the door for demonic possession, 3) fall prey to natural catastrophes, such as fire, when the charms/fetishes no longer work or require "recharging", 4) apoplectic fits, 5) dementia/insanity, and 6) early death from "natural causes", such as heart attack, certain cancers, etc.

[**Note**: *Make appointment for August 26]*

AUGUST 21, 1977:

I had a scheduled session with Jane and her mother on August 26, but Jane's mother called my office today to inform me that her daughter was in ICU for a minor heart attack. Jane's mother also told me that heart attacks among the young in her family are common. This known fact, plus Jane's morbid obesity, poor diet, lack of sleep (or disturbed sleep) and melancholy are all reasonable factors that could have brought this MI about.

After my last appointment for the day, I stopped by the hospital on my way home after picking up a bouquet of flowers. Jane was still in ICU with her parents and younger brother by her side. After her mother introduced me to her husband and son, I engaged her husband in some trivial chit-chat. While engaged in our conversation, Jane went into cardiac arrest. As soon as the hospital STAT team came into the room, her vital signs returned to normal. As the hospital staff began to direct us out the door so that they could attend to Jane, she woke up and called for her mother. Her parents and brother approached her side while I stood by the door looking on to see if she was OK. She looked up into her parents faces and said, "Mommy, Daddy, I can no longer live this way. I love you. Goodbye."

Though she was perfectly stable after the brief emergency, I stood there and watched her face completely change. Her eyes, which were intently focused on the faces of her family suddenly glassed over and her urgent expression relaxed into one with no sign of cognizance.

She had just left her body, there is no doubt in my mind that I was witness to the excursion of her soul.

Just as I was marveling over everything I watched transpire over the previous thirty minutes or so, she went into cardiac arrest again, only this time, she could not be revived. Without her soul returning to her body, she died, leaving her soul marooned in a distant land, and hopefully, one that she enjoyed.

Note: Research a potential new category of deictic phenomena: spook apparitions and ghosts.

OTHER PASTIMES

A Flower

Against the horizon of sand and sky,
I saw a flower upon a beach.
I stood alone, and wondered why,
Such flora bloomed from within my reach.
The white pedals drew me
Closer to its form.
It was lovely . . .
Beautiful . . .
Fragrant..
Warm.

A Moth

In through my window flew a moth so frail,
In from the night it searched, lest if fail.
For alas, upon its wings of weary flight
Did it spy from a distance, my bedroom light.

At the candle, above the dancing flame,
Out from the darkness of night it came.
No longer its shadow dips and flutters
Against the stage of my window's shutters.

Gothic Desire

I am left here, bound to the night,
Hurting through this darkened silence,
My heart so sad and empty,
This desire betrayed.
A tragic abyss,
Hurled away,
Yet I still long for
Your touch so warm.

Oceanic Aerosol

I fell down
Crushed my heart into the beach,
Pockets full of sand.

Gulls laughing overhead
Like a chorus of children playing
With some contraband.

"NO SWIMMING ALLOWED"
The yellow placard read,
Swearing and smoking banned.

It was a summer when
Sea Monkeys were still legal
And parents had the upper hand.

I got up
My lips sprayed by the crashing waves,
My body tanned.

With another murder
All things point to heaven,
So said the weatherman.

Lament of a Fallen Angel

It will be yonder when our twain souls shall meet,
The single essence of one meaningful 'trick or treat'.
Past shadowed silhouettes of crosses that still stand,
I can't eulogize cemeteries the church took as my land.

The shadows of death that hang from midnight spires,
Fill the night with the silence of discrete hell fires.
In an age when the light separates the blackest of night,
How the pawns of Beelzebub must faint from the sight!

The depths of my vile soul scream out in pain,
What forgiveness shall I receive if I fall once again?
The knell of Hell's bells becomes louder still,
As I balance myself from the edge of this windowsill.

As I peer over this city's self-destruction,
I see much death, but also resurrection.
Why desecrate the city streets with my brain,
When there may be much for me to gain?

I suppose I am a trick, perhaps even the treat,
Though I'm someone you wouldn't want to meet.
I live in the darkness while you live in the light,
I thirst for evil, while you starve for what's right.

Hell's bells—they are a reminder to me,
That you get to live once, and then it's eternity.
In the darkest hours, which I fear the most,
You still have time before you give up the ghost.

Civil Duty and Circus Tents

They bruised his lip,
But the organ grinder starts up again,
Only now, even the monkey
Is loosening its grip
On the door to the loot
To avoid being stripped
Of the money
His keeper spends on fruit.

He's a "John Doe",
Like a comedian out of work,
He knows he's not a jerk
Yet in the public's eyes,
He's paid to know
Between right and wrong
And to break out into song
When truth comprises the show.

He's a magic man;
A master of coins and cards,
But even he can't protect
The secrets he guards.
When left alone
And completely unchecked,
He's still a man that loses
To tricks, lies and ruses.

She's a politician,
She once meant well,
But now her wealth
Has made a bed in Hell.

A woman on a mission,
We drink to her health,
This modern Jezebel—
Now where's the magician?

So, we sing with the monkey
And laugh with the fool
And give all our money
To those that rule,
But at least the magic man
Still understands
That mirrors and smoke
Don't make it a joke.

Balloon

I recollect my childhood
Like a sweet morsel melting in my mouth,
Skipping school and skimming stones,
The days were long and slow.
Yet no matter how resourceful,
The memory still aches within my bones.
When you whistled that muddled tune,
I was the puddle you rode your bicycle through.
Among the balloons, colorful and carefree,
I was the tiny bubble smiling among the crowd,
Designed to make you stop, and notice me,
But I was avoided—you were just too proud.
I've lived my life as though I'd live forever,
Yet feared impending death with every breath.
I trace these words because I cannot surrender
To a live worth living, which yields to death.
So, I had no choice but to cut the tether.
I'm not the man I made, but a little boy,
Still clinging to the rocks, braving the icy waves,
Waiting for you to reach down and rescue me,
To set me on your shoulders, free of the sea,
But this little room that you've locked me in,
Keeps me wanting for what might have been.

Friends

I've traveled now for many miles,
It felt so good to see the smiles
Of friends who never left my mind
When they were so very far away.
From the golden light
Of the approaching dawn,
Until twilight when the sun is gone,
I'll treasure every passing day.

Sentimental Incense

I've been wondering about what you said,
Was it something you meant,
Or is it something you mean?
I'll take the chance if you take the blame,
But I cannot accept the flowers you sent.

The accumulation of leaves
Piling up as a layer over the others,
Like old thoughts of our past years,
Now rest idle like the empty gossip
Of inner-city ghetto mothers.

In this autumn breeze I sense the end
To another romance birthed in Spring,
The blue disappears from the sudden gray
Of another October sky
That doesn't remind me of anything.

Your shadow no longer lingers
Like a dove hovering above our bed,
Too many disappointments,
Like unwanted children of the powerful
And young teenagers still unwed.

Yet, it's still a new morning,
And each day brings the promise of hope.
I chose to shake off the memories
That have for so long hung around
Like the noose of a hangman's rope.

Each new wave brings sand from the deeps
And pulls the filth back into the sea.
Everyone deserves a new beginning
And I am hoping and wishing
There is still one more left for me.

Nothing Can Stop Us Now

Nothing can stop us now,
Standing at the beach,
Wading in the waves
Like a newlywed
With her life ahead
Like the signs
That let us pass
Along the way.

Nothing can stop us now,
With this road ahead,
Climbing mountains,
Crossing rivers,
Giving life
And burying
The dead
Along the way.

Nothing can stop us now
With dreams in our head,
Throwing stones,
Snapping matches,
Burning bridges
And passing through
The tolls ahead
Along the way.

Nothing can stop us now
With the stars widespread,
Like jewels hanging in the sky
Reflected
In wishing wells
Well fed
With copper coins
Along the way.

The Ocean's Wrath

I've set my sails for happier seas,
As I leave behind those sadder shores.
The harbor I seek lies far away
Beyond any charted, man-made course.

The waves that beat against my hull,
Carry my ship from side to side,
With the wheel held firmly in my hands,
I will not yield to the ever-changing tide.

The anchor that grasps firm and strong,
Will keep me from drifting into the shoals,
But should I sink into the depths unknown,
I will never forsake my worthy goals.

Though I sail through storms day and night,
And I am denied food, water and rest,
Time and tide will not take their hold
Upon this oaken wheel against my chest.

The ocean is both a gateway to life and death,
As my ship traverses a salty path.
Though I rejoice in the eye of the storm,
Hell hath no fury like the ocean's wrath.

September Song

The autumn wind that sounds like fear,
Is lost in the footsteps that bring you near.
The rain that drives my hair down, down,
Begins to make my hope in you drown.

Look at me and do not pretend,
That you'll love me until the end.
There's something ambiguous in your eye,
When the truth turns out to be a lie.

When you walked from me backwards,
I wasn't offended by your words,
When they found their mark inside,
It was the thought that you implied.

There's something noble about a broken heart,
That clings to the past but never saves,
Now that all of your words fall apart,
And fall into the pits of open graves.

Soon it will be winter, cold and gray,
But still, I am here for you—I will stay.
Spring will be around the corner next year
And even without you, I'll still be near.

Then

It was summer then,
When
The grass was greener
And the trees were higher;
The sky bluer
Than any sky today,
And all of this
Was legal
Then.

We watched storms
When
The rain was cleaner
And with nights on fire,
There were fewer
Than there are today,
But all of this
Was legal
Then.

It was different then,
When
We were leaner
And more inspired.
The nights were cooler
Than any night today
And all of this
Was legal
Then.

Then
The clouds came in
Again.
I became a dreamer
But without desire—
A pursuer
Of all the ones that got away.
Now it's winter
Again.

Then
The path was clear
But I've lost my way
And my best friend.
I've read it in books
There's always an end.
How I wish
It was summer
Then.

American Mexico

When the siren sounds, I sit up,
Nervous, tense and sweating.
Hands press up against the glass,
My eyes search the streets
With memories I'm still regretting . . .

I sit like an Indian on my bed,
Cross-legged and transfixed,
Like a nun taking the wine and bread
Beneath her bedroom crucifix.

When the lightning strikes, I lay low,
Like all the cattle before a storm.
Choking blood from a baby's veins,
I'm relieved I even made it through
A doctor's quest for sucking brains
Through a needle and a plastic tube.

Day changes like a flash into night,
I want to run, but I need to fight.
I watched the gore a mother bore,
Like priest's pouring out the blood
From a supper that they all abhor,
Drowning their ignorance in a flood.

I was there—I watched it all—
Forced to watch their tiny fingers fall.
I watched the murder but when I asked why,
I was admonished for turning my head to cry.
They ridiculed me for being weak,
While they justified their damn technique.

There are no sirens for the lost,
No beacon for the forgotten.
With all the blood I saw
There's just not enough cotton.
So, I bow my head against the glass,
Astonished by such an overflow
Of all the fetuses, that like me pass
Into the rivers of Mexico.

Dreams

Silhouettes dance upon the wall in a kind of symphony,
From the flickering flame of light through my keyhole.
Like a puppet on your hand, enslaved by spirits of the night,
Dreams reign, and for a time, I am left without a soul.

I fear the death of sleep, as temporary as it always is,
For I am enslaved in bondage to sights of such misery.
Is this a reflection of a life that never once tasted bliss,
Or am I captivated in the palms of some witchery?

I'm living the dream! But the dream is a nightmare—
What have I done to see hell before I am even dead?
What does it mean, what does it all forebear
If am cheated of life from the hours slept in bed?

Why has the joy of living left me to the hours of the night,
Where I am tortured and struck with such demonic force?
Throughout the daylight hours, the Lord is still my Light,
But I'm too worn out to fight when the night takes its course.

Certainly, there is a purpose, I must remind myself,
For nothing makes sense without a meaning.
Perhaps these ghosts and visions I cannot explain
Are what makes me feel like I'm only dreaming.

Infinite Sadness

I stand before our bedroom window,
Looking down, down, down.
The rain outside and my tears inside
Make me want to drown, drown, drown.

Sometimes this room gets kind of empty;
No presence in the shadows of the light.
I think about this loveless situation,
Sitting alone by myself again tonight.

Curtains steal the air from my window,
As the night weeps upon the glass.
Colors bleed along the streets below
As I stare, and let the hours pass.

Tomorrow comes, but we're not there to see it;
Another day is missed because of you.
I watch the signs in godless fascination,
Hoping for something to get me through.

In our youth, it was us against the world,
But tonight, the past has become a stranger.
You're still as fickle as a high school girl;
There's no thrill in living without danger.

Farming

I farm the fallow land
Like the words you use
To plow my back:
Churchyard lies,
Screen door flies,
Upstairs cries,
And the alibis
You make to your friends
When I am away.

Iron

She thinks I'm made of iron, but I'm only made of clay.
I'm the thief in the night that steals her dreams away.
Since the blame is mine, I need no redemption,
Our world is breaking apart, there is no question.
If you are beloved of someone else, someone dear,
There will be disappointment, there will be grief,
But it isn't the lingering nights of loneliness I fear,
But the impending kiss of death that is a thief.
Her skin is porcelain white and her black hair like silk,
Her floral fragrance intoxicates and relieves me of all guilt.
By myself, her shadow encompasses me in an iron will,
A gentle, warm summer breeze that removes the chill.

Eden

I cannot listen to your lies,
I cannot show grace and sympathize,
For my final hope dies
If I stare into your eyes,
And let them hypnotize.

I cannot feel the warmth
With the cold touch of your hand.
Eden has lain for a thousand years
To be our promised land,
But is now stained by our tears.

When I stare into your icy stare,
Like a child before a statue.
I cannot see the light,
I'm surrounded by night,
And with no exit to pass through.

Eden has lain for a thousand years,
But now the meadows are a flood,
The plains are empty,
The seas full of salt
And our hands are full of blood.

Fanned by the flames,
I cannot see the light,
It is me the world blames,
Leaving me in disgrace
And obscured by the night.

You gave me a false embrace!
Now we must hide our heads in shame,
Like sheep lead to the slaughter,
Like the infants of our future
Destroyed without a name.

These broad lands had lain in peace
For a thousand years,
But now it is all a wasteland
With no water
Except for our tears.

Together, you and I must go,
Leaving these lands plaited with life.
We exchanged eternal bliss for just one bite;
A lick and a promise from a fruit
Forbidden to a husband and wife.

The serpent sings his song
Like a siren marooned at sea,
But it will not be so long
Before he pays for this wrong
In the abyss of eternity.

Yet, beyond the gates of fire
Guarded by force and cruel might,
We have a Savior who
Will bring us back to these lands
Lain in hope and eternal light.

Hourglass

Yesterday,
My countenance fell,
Like an oaken bucket
That was plunged down a well –
Like a diver going down
Into the green, green sea –
Like a tornado
Of repression
That drove all of my
Childhood dreams
Into the ground.

Today,
It takes everything I know
To be brave and strong,
In spite of the fact
That no one gets along,
Like magnets that repel
And waves that sink and swell
Against a ship lost at sea
Fighting the wind and waves
Of nothing that saves
Drifters such as you and me.

Tomorrow,
Is already yesterday,
And the cycle begins again.
Like all the stories
With the very same end,
We rewind our past
For something to last
Beyond the sands
That no one understands
Why they pass so fast
Through this hourglass.

What is time,
But an end to the means
In forming a memory,
An enemy without a face
Except for the ghosts
That invade our space
In dreamy scenes
Reminding us of
What we could have,
And should have been,
   . . . and without machines.

I hold this hourglass
In my hands
Like a future
That might have been,
But the sands
Pass quickly
And cover the bottom
As though I've already
Been forgotten . . .
How fast our lives pass by
Before we wonder why.

I could reverse it,
Being the cheat that I am,
But time stops for nothing,
Like the sands blowing
On a hot Sahara day . . .
Like a hurricane
Caught in a traffic jam,
Time isn't slowing,
It cannot betray,
So, I watch the hourglass,
Bury memories into sand.

Always

As this month
Ends today,
Blue skies
Turn gray
And the mountains
In my mirror
Fade away.

The road ahead
Receives me
With quiet dignity,
But the blur of trees
And passing cars
Affects me
Differently.

I dream
Of sleeping forever
Among wires,
Television
And radio –
Sad music
In stereo . . .

There's nothing
I remember
When with
Friends like you,
But Chris is dead,
Curtis died
And my father too.

Each year
Gets harder
To appreciate
Much as I
Once did
As a carefree
Ignorant kid.

I cry no more—
The tears
Are hard to come by
These days.
Yet as I die more each year
I'll still have you
With me
Always.

Transient Mirrors

The Autumn leaves are falling,
Another Summer lies in the past.
I hear angry people calling—
They're sick and tired of being asked.

Ultimatums are boring,
As the world continues snoring.
Here I am, standing on the beach,
Alone, happy and out of reach.

There are rain clouds in the sky,
With waves rising over my feet.
They keep asking me why I try
When the answer is in defeat.

When it's raining and the skies are black,
And when I can hear the thunder roll,
I just need to see the lighting crack
To feel anything alive within my soul.

It may just be fascination with death
And food for the few, so it seems,
Today, with so many smoking meth
In front of television screens.

I don't pretend it isn't so—
Why this weakness—no one knows?
Vacant, faceless voices on the phone
Bring no comfort to those alone.

So, cover your ears and shade your eyes,
Your world remains out of reach,
But for me, I will watch the skies
Kicking shells off the beach.

Roman

Another ruined romance,
Another lowering glance,
Yet they despise the circumstance,—
A virtue without reverence.
They do not fear this decadence—
This rotting renaissance,
So, now kiss me, my Grace
As I feel thy cold embrace.

Under a dark veil you hide,
Darkest delights and insight:
A paper golden star for me,
As the ice cream melts in my hand,
A final gift of yourself to me
But you like it better when I stand.

I fear thy spiteful gaze
Through this moonlight's haze.
I despise thy mournful face
Beyond the veil of black lace.
I fear thy deepest gaze;
I loathe thy mournful face.
There's no joy or praise
In you black lords of disgrace.

I see your endless pride
In darkened candlelight.
Your hunger grows fast—
This flame inside your chest.
You breathe so close to me,
Your curse is bathed in years.
You plunge inside of me
An ocean of tragic tears.

Under a dark veil you hide
In lunar light of black light.
I smell your winter icy scent—
Foul water in the moonlight.
You speak in tongues of fire,
Yet you never knew my name,
I'm another sad desire,
You're my curse and my flame.

And in my evanescent dream,
My final dying Grace,
With gray ashen light so dim,
I hope to God He hides your face.
I'm much older now,
And full of regret,
Because it was your winning smile
That I can never forget.

The past still towers
Over me like a ghost
Because what your Grace ever saw in me,
I cannot unsee what you've done,
But what was done in secret
Will be revealed to everyone.

Another Holocaust

Eyes peer over a windowsill
Searching another midnight sky.
Fingers clasp together in a prayer
Without really knowing why.
The stars shine,
And they shine so hard.

You erase the memories with
The smell of death in the air.
No more good times, like the times
You had with the bones lying there.
The rain falls,
And it falls so hard.

History repeats itself,
You read the writing on the wall,
But still, you make the same mistakes
That make civilizations fall.
The wind blows,
And it blows so hard.

Butterflies

She tastes like cinnamon rain,
And her hair pours over me as silk.
She has made me hers and I'm her swain,
Like a babe drunk on mother's milk.

She walks in grace and I'm in love.
Promises hang higher in bluer skies.
She walks in grace and I'm in love.
Rainbows give way to butterflies.

Her eyes shimmer like silver,
And she calls to me this night!
I bow my head and I shiver,
Her kiss sets my soul alight!

She walks in grace and I'm in love,
Like the ocean waves that swell and rise.
She walks in grace and I'm in love,
Another rainbow among butterflies.

In Green Pastures

As the robin craves the summertime
In which to hide its smock of red,
So I crave your hands of comfort
In which to bury my head.

In the green pastures where I wept,
Below the trees where the robin sings
Of all the promises I could have kept
Had I stayed away from worldly things.

Bitter were the tears I cried for you
When I felt so far, far away.
Only for a brief moment did I turn from you,
For a brief moment did I turn away.

Then in your great loving-kindness
You came and you gathered me,
For how was I to fulfill a life
With a heart locked in agony.

Goodbye green pastures, I leave you now
My weary life ends only to begin.
Farewell sad skies and fallow ground,
I will never visit you again.

The Mist Amang the Heather

'Twas a cold night the fell o'er the town,
When a lass lost in the wood was never found.
Yet, yonder in the heather, a mist befalls,
So dense that no one could hear her calls.

She stepped upon a path that all knew well,
A path down by where the rivers swell.
Led she was, like sheep to the slaughter
To suffer at the hands of earth and water.

Out from the dark, he reached for her dress
Then drew her close to his ready caress,
But she ran, she pleaded, she cried, she fell
Down to the soft ground in the fury of hell.

To this day on cold and rainy nights,
After all in town have put out their lights,
Cries for help arise out o'er the weather
Throughout the mist amang the heather.

There Was a Garden Once

There once was a garden
That treasured its seed,
But there was no pardon,
When all turned to weed.

The choices were made,
Then remorse and regret.
Now the stars are arrayed,
Like a tattered net.

No garden can exist
Without a farmer,
Any more than a fist
Can without armor.

Forever caught between
Acts of evil and good,
Some will die unseen,
And others will wish they could.

With retreat, there is no return,
You only receive what you earn.
Isolation is not a choice,
One person has no voice.

Borrowed strength,
Lost innocence,
And a man's years in length
Amount to wickedness.

But a faithful man
Is a vicious one of routines,
He understands—
He knows what it means.

Protected on all fronts,
Dusk to dawn,
There was a Garden once,
But now it's gone.

Like shadows and dreams,
Promises and schemes,
We let the Garden
Become a burden.

Now we look back
When looking ahead,
But all is black
And the Garden is dead.

The one seed
Still stuck in our throat
Is the only one we need
And it is Hope.

October

Join me in the blackness of the hour,
Of mid-October's graceful falling,
When leaves yield to an autumn shower,
And my past is forever calling.
Memorial is my agony!
Remorse and regret, my hell to pay!
Partners in crime, I must yield to thee,
And plead for mercy on Judgment Day.
Evil breathes the same dark spirit now,
October remains unmoved and cold.
I lie with death sealed upon my brow,
And a memory one cannot behold.
No anthem, or prayer, or incense rise,
Desires, or dreams, or longing hearts,
Can remove the dull coins from my eyes,
Or relieve my soul of the devil's darts.
The common passer will peruse the tomb,
And pity the poor words engraved in black,
Of wayward deeds and a fitting doom,
For one so imprisoned upon his back.

The Most Beautiful Suicide

(In memory of Evelyn McHale)

One of nine,
Yet one of mine,
She didn't need to die
Leaping from the sky.

Where was I in all of this,
A note sealed with a kiss,
Begging for cremation
Without any consolation.

Her little black pocketbook
Held the suicidal note.
New York City shook
Waiting to read what she wrote.

All I remember is her face,
Beautiful and sad
Yet so full of grace
It really made me mad.

Soft and sad, lost and lonely
But no lonelier than any angel.
This beautiful girl isn't the only
One without a story to tell.

Tonight, as the rain falls
Like a curtain on a closing play,
Our interest withdraws
From what the papers say.

Your beauty in the photograph—
86 floors had no effect on you.
I hold tightly your last paragraph
Wishing that I once knew you.

Intervals

Though my body rests, and slumber robs me of my thought,
My spirit never sleeps through the dreams it tries to blot.
Your spell that overcomes me by banishing the hours,
Enslaves me to a world where I am captured by your powers.

I yield my desires to the pillow beneath my head,
And exchange my appetites for a world without dread.
From a thing unseen and a presence, I cannot feel,
I sense the phantom from the rest I find so surreal.

Though the nights deny me fleeting pleasures of the day,
And the constellations refuse me their cheerful array,
The visions that are legion, and yet remain unknown,
Are the sweetest hours I spend, mingled with thine own.

Another Day at the Races

I despise the rainbow you raise like a flag,
It's more like the colors of a grocery bag.
Broken lives pile up like wedding rings
Upon an altar of unwanted things.
Colorless corpses floating down a sink
Into a river full of filth with a stink,
Yet you split hairs over creeds and races
And turn away from these poor little faces.

The media is desperate to inform you
Of the real issues you can choose to ignore,
Your Sunday morning breath reminds you
This is what you slept in late for.
The news has ransomed you once again,
Another effort to set you free,
But you've buried your sleeping head
In a mire of sensuality.

Respect your elders hanging on strings
Like puppets controlled by someone higher,
Cut those tethers that hold you down
And throw the ropes into the fire.
Follow your dreams and grow some wings,
And leave the shadows far behind,
Don't let another generation drown
In the nameless river of bloody wine.

Forgotten

After I've been forgotten
And all the eyes have dried,
Things will be as they were
As though I never even died.

It is a lonely situation—
No one can hear me scream at all,
As I suffer this damnation,
Lying naked up against the wall.

Children play upon my silent tomb
Throwing pebbles at my stone,
There may not be much room in here,
But it's all I have to call my own.

Flowers have stopped coming by
In the hands of someone I once knew,
And forever I will have to ask why
I had to be separated from you.

I suppose I never really listened
And it seems like I never learned,
That once we have departed,
Once called, we cannot return.

Send in the Clowns

Their eyes are empty and full of disgrace,
They yearn for the smile of a happy face,
And I can see it in their eyes,
False alibis,
Hopeless dreams,
Screams...

Life is good when sad clowns feel great,
But only with a heart beating full of hate.
The traces in their cheeks, forged by tears,
Reflect the abuse of childhood years,
A hole in their chest, where a heart used to be,
A twinkle of the eye, now a nobody.

Tiny little crystals of death bring pleasure
When there is no promise of a treasure
That will remove the truth from the lies,
Like the way paint covers all in disguise—
The lonely nights and rainy towns—
Oh, just send in the clowns...

Matthew 6:34

I awoke again this morning
To play the troubles
Of another day.
They come without warning
And there is nothing
You can say.

It's raining in the meadow,
And the people
Have gone back to town.
My life is a shadow
When there is
No one else around.

The stars fall
Forever the night,
And still, I walk the clay.
The darkness gives
Way to light—
Another troubled day.

Star Blood

Weep . . .
Raindrops, or grains of sand.
Pain . . .
It's all we understand.
Truth . . .
Knowledge is such sorrow.
Time . . .
Today is already tomorrow.
Passion . . .
Like youth, passes away.
Trust . . .
Betrays all you ever say.
Laugh . . .
A breath away from crying.
Honesty . . .
As cheap as your lying.
Faith . . .
I dine on the sins I've forgiven.
Hope . . .
Is all I have ever given.

The Twilight of This Evening

The twilight of this evening
Is splintered in color
Outside my window.
Snow falls like manna from heaven
And the branches groan
From the weight of the snow.

Where is the warmth of the sun
In all of this?
I cannot see it, yet it hovers still,
Like a beacon of faith
That with every summer sunrise
Floods my windowsill.

There's a sort of remorse
And a kind of regret
That these storms bring.
The hope that each
Snowflake carries,
Points to another Spring.

So, I sit back in my chair,
Watching the snowflakes fall
In fresh white layers,
Like the whispering
Of children
Going up to heaven in prayers.

My Verdict

My verdict is law,
It has passed.
Now your judgement
Draws near.

Yet I get this feeling
God can change everything,
Like how the rain
Brings life
And beauty back
In its healing.

My verdict is law
But it lacks devotion.
It incites fear
And kneeling
Before choirs singing,
But more from pain—
Almost childlike,
Cloaked in black
While kneeling.
God protect me
From this hate.

My verdict is law,
But what is yours?
Resurrect me
From this fate,
And remove this pain—
It's as cold as ice,
Yet hot as hell,
And unappealing.

My verdict is law!
Isn't it?
Lifting myself
From the silence
Of a wasted life
Taken from me—
Like one
Without a choice,
Thoughts lost
Within myself—
Quiet and lonely
And without a voice.

My verdict
Seems less
Important
Like everyone knows.
So, I'll take the needle—
The vein seems
less a margin
while my arm goes stiff.
In this sense
Each vein glows.

My verdict
Cannot be!
It's nothing
to do with you
And nothing
to do with me.
It's to do with
Forgiveness,
Remorse, regret
And mercy.
Let my verdict
Be on you.

Wind

The body is the scar
Of the mind;
A truth that burns
With approaching age.
The wind that blows
Through my hair so fine,
Is the force that turns
Another page.

My Love

My love,
Why do you check the sky?
There are no clouds,
No birds to fly.

My love,
Why do you watch the sea?
There are no waves
To cover your feet.

My love,
Why do you bury the dead?
There is no sand,
Only blood instead.

My love,
Why do you look for me?
You cannot join me
In eternity.

Bydand

"A Gordon! A Gordon!" was their battle cry,
A shout of terror in the blood red sky.
Gordons of Gight, Lochinvar and Kenmure
'Gored down' the land, once godly and pure.

Feuding, indebted, murderers and murdered;
Robbers, ill-mannered, and poorly worded;
All this and more were their barbaric lot,
Except for the battles that they bravely fought.

In spite of themselves, some goodness prevailed
When upon the scaffolds some Gordons were nailed.
Tollbooth prisoners, martyrs and exiles,
Gordons became saints from those mocking trials.

Though time heals all wounds and some fade away,
The memories of the land will forever remain.
From the Clan Chieftain to the lowliest of serfs,
A Gordon is a Gordon—a name he proudly serves.

"Scotland the Brave" is played livelier still
On the pipes of a Gordon when played high on a hill.
When time passes and, in the earth, we are laid,
May the chant, "A Gordon! A Gordon!" never fade.

Last Thoughts

He looked down without fear,
But it was too far to fall.
With the wind twisting his hair,
His skin began to crawl.

Among a stack of photographs,
There was a bluish flame.
From the smoke, a child laughed,
And whispered out his name.

The blade shimmered in his hand,
As he cried out a single word –
One a priest would understand,
And the Devil find absurd.

There is no forgiveness when
No sacrifice can be made;
First the quest departs, then
The desire begins to fade.

Who will save the losing from the lost,
And wipe the tear from their eye?
He should have first counted the cost
Before he bid one last goodbye.

www.ingramcontent.com/pod-product-compliance
Lightning Source LLC
Chambersburg PA
CBHW062012220426
43662CB00010B/1300